But that Thy blood was shed for me,
To rid my soul of one dark blot,
With many a conflict, many a doubt,
Sight, riches, heal-ing of the mind,
Wilt welcome, pardon, cleanse, relieve;

O Lamb of God, I come, I come!
O Lamb of God, I come, I come!
O Lamb of God, I come, I come!
O Lamb of God, I come, I come!
O Lamb of God, I come, I come!

ENDORSEMENTS FOR *HYMN RESTORATION*

We sing hymns not because they are old, but because they are great and contain so much of our theology. So, a big thanks to you, Dino, for helping to save a very important part of our Christian history, and may God bless you, my friend, in this special effort.

BILL GAITHER
Composer, Producer, Director

There is nothing like the classic hymns of the Christian faith, which are so rich in doctrine, to lead us in worship. They inspire us to rightly revere Almighty God as we lift our voices and declare the truth of who He is and all He has done for us. I am grateful to Dino for compiling this great collection of hymns and for his tireless work in exalting the name of Jesus.

DR. CHARLES STANLEY
Senior Pastor of First Baptist Atlanta
Founder and President of In Touch Ministries

Dino is a personal friend whose love for God and His people is infectious. Nowhere is this more evident than in his exquisite music. And his music now reaches a crescendo in this beautiful, meaningful volume of hymns. Enjoy!

ANNE GRAHAM LOTZ

HYMN
RESTORATION

101
Treasured Hymns
with Devotions

DINO & CHERYL KARTSONAKIS

Nordskog Publishing inc.

Ventura, California

Hymn Restoration: 101 Treasured Hymns with Devotions
by Dino and Cheryl Kartsonakis
Copyright © 2018 by Dino and Cheryl Kartsonakis
Second printing, June 2019

Capitalization has occasionally been modified from the original.
Photos of the Kartsonakises are by Meadows Images.
Back cover hymn writer portraits are PD-US, thanks to Wikimedia Commons.
Unless otherwise indicated, all graphic illustrations are PD-US, thanks to Wikimedia Commons.

ISBN: 978-1-946497-44-4

Cover Design: Dave Danielson, Danielson Design
Interior Design, Managing Editor: Michelle Shelfer, benediction.biz
Project Facilitator: Christina Kartsonakis
Proofreading: Cheryl Geyer

Printed in the United States of America by Jostens, Inc.

Published by

2716 Sailor Avenue, Ventura, California 93001
1-805-642-2070 • 1-805-276-5129
NordskogPublishing.com

THIS BOOK IS DEDICATED to our Lord and Savior Jesus Christ,
with thankfulness for the music He placed
within the hearts of these excellent hymn composers.
They have ministered to the world through their songs.
We are also thankful for our ears to hear and hearts to worship.

Be filled with the Spirit;
speaking to yourselves in psalms and hymns
and spiritual songs,
singing and making melody in your heart to the Lord.
(Ephesians 5:18–19)

Photo by Paul M. Walsh

William Franklin Graham, Jr. (1918–2018)

WE WISH TO HONOR the ministry of Dr. Billy Graham that
brought Christ's saving power to the world. Many of these
hymns were sung in his crusades around the world to
prepare the hearts of the people to receive the Word of God
as ministered by Dr. Billy Graham.

As publishers, Christians, and hymn lovers, Jerry and Gail Nordskog are so pleased to be partnering with the incomparable Dino and Cheryl Kartsonakis to bring you this collection of beloved hymns!

ABOUT DINO AND CHERYL

Dino Kartsonakis is known as one of the world's premier pianists, a title aptly given. From Carnegie Hall to the honor of performing inside the Tower of David, Jerusalem, Dino has captured the world with his unique talent, stellar performances, and exceptional showmanship.

Kartsonakis is a Grammy Award winner for playing on the soundtrack of the movie *The Apostle*. He was nominated for "Chariots of Fire," and is an eight-time Dove Award winner and Tele Award winner for *Miracles*, filmed at David's Tower in Jerusalem.

Dino's talent and performance prowess all started at the tender age of three, when he sat at an upright piano and played the hymn "At the Cross" that he heard that morning at church. He grew into his talents and later studied music at The King's College, piano at The Julliard School in New York City, at The

Munich Conservatory in Germany, and the Conservatory of Fontainebleau in France, where he studied under the famous concert pianist Arthur Rubinstein.

Cheryl has sung and Dino has played concerts in his famed style in such places as Russia, Japan, China, and Israel, to name a few—also Carnegie Hall, the Hollywood Bowl, Lincoln Center, and many other prestigious venues nationwide, performing for many dignitaries. He toured extensively in Europe under the auspices of the United States Army Special Services. He was featured in evangelist Kathryn Kuhlman's *I Believe in Miracles* television show on CBS Television Network, working with Kuhlman for seven years.

Aside from touring the world, Dino has made countless network television appearances since the age of sixteen, including the highly rated talk show *The Dino Show*, produced and hosted by Dino and Cheryl. For over twenty-five years they wowed audiences in over two hundred countries with a variety of celebrity guests as well as performances by Dino and Cheryl.

Most recently, Dino had the distinction of playing at Israel's 70th Birthday Celebration Concert with the Jerusalem Philharmonic Orchestra the night before the U.S. Embassy opened in Jerusalem, with Pat Boone singing and serving as MC.

Cheryl Kartsonakis has performed as a vocalist for the past twenty-five years, entertaining audiences around the world alongside her husband. She is also the designer of many of the gorgeous costumes and sets in the Kartsonakis concert extravaganzas.

In 2007, Dino and Cheryl opened Dino's 24Karrot Cake Company and Cafe, located in Branson, Missouri, also shipping their "Celebrity Favorite" cakes nationwide.

Dino and Cheryl are not only world-renowned entertainers, but they are also husband and wife. Dino and Cheryl share two daughters, Christina and Cherie, and are grandparents to Cherie and her husband Steve's daughters, Lauren and Alexandra.

PUBLISHER'S WORD

And He hath put a new song in my mouth, even praise unto our God: many shall see it, and fear, and shall trust in the LORD. (Psalm 40:3)

In June 2017, my beloved wife, Gail Grace, launched her first book, *Hearts of Purpose: Real-life stories about ten ordinary women doing extraordinary things for the Glory of God*, at the International Christian Retail Show in Cincinnati.

When the show ended, we packed up and proceeded to Dr. Ken Ham's Creation Museum and the Noah's Ark replica in Kentucky. From there we traveled to Branson, Missouri, where a friend of ours facilitated a very special meeting with Dino Kartsonakis and his wife Cheryl, who live there. Gail and I met the Kartsonakises for lunch on July 3rd, prior to Independence Day, and further visited with them three more times that week, as we became instant friends on that summer trip in 2017. We also joined them there for the grand opening of Dino's 24Karrot Cake & Coffee Company and Cafe in downtown Branson, and again for one of Dino's concert events in March 2018. Gratefully, we discovered that we are kindred spirits.

In May 2018, Gail and I toured the Holy Land during the 70th anniversary of modern-day Israel and the celebration of the U.S. Embassy move to Jerusalem. Dino and Cheryl were part of that tour as well, bringing their musical gifts to the whole special tour experience.

Dino called me upon the homegoing of the Rev. Dr. Billy Graham, asking me if we were interested in publishing a hymnal with some of the hymns Cliff Barrows and George Beverly Shea sang at Dr. Graham's Crusades, along with older classic hymns. I immediately and enthusiastically affirmed to him, YES, YES, YES! Like Dino (and many other Christians), Gail and I always loved the old gospel hymns by the Biblical hymn writers and musicians. Yet many or even most of the churches in America have put hymns on the back burner or some even in archives. Many younger-generation churchgoers have not been exposed to the great hymns of the past, so full of anointed Scriptures.

So we mutually decided almost instantly that we wanted to come out with a new hymnal for today's churches to place into the hands of as many congregants as would embrace it.

Hence, in March of 2018, we covenanted to work together in bringing to YOU, the reader, singer, and praise worshiper, this hymn book, *Hymn Restoration: 101 Treasured Hymns.* Shortly after that decision, the Kartsonakis and Nordskog families decided with pleasure to add a devotional page to accompany each and every song in our hymn book, which Cheryl has researched and lovingly written.

These classic hymns from many years ago are overflowing with Bible Scripture, and all of us need to sing Holy Scriptures as often as we can—constantly—not just in church services, but in our homes together. We now introduce to that younger generation of Christians who have experienced mostly modern-day music in their worship services these Holy Spirit inspired hymns! Those already familiar with the hymns will also cherish the revival of these time-honored treasures.

We praise and thank the Lord for His attributes of justice and love, who gave us beautiful music to joyfully exalt and worship Him, and we are further refreshed by Cheryl's accompanying devotionals as we honor Christ our King.

Let this be a new season of *hymn restoration* in America and all over the world. As hymn writer Isaac Watts once wrote, "Joy to the world, the Lord is come! Let earth receive her King!"

This is the day which the LORD *hath made; we will rejoice and be glad in it.* (Psalm 118:24)

The LORD *is my strength and song, and He is become my salvation.* (Exodus 15:2)

Rejoice in the Lord alway: and again I say, Rejoice! (Philippians 4:4)

My soul magnifies the Lord,
and my spirit rejoices in God my Savior.

For He has regarded the low estate of His servant;
surely, from now on all generations will call me blessed.

For He who is mighty has done great things for me,
and holy is His name.

His mercy is on those who fear Him
from generation to generation.

He has shown strength with His arm;
He has scattered the proud
in the imagination of their hearts.

He has pulled down the mighty from their thrones
and exalted those of low degree.

He has filled the hungry with good things,
and the rich He has sent away empty.

He has helped His servant Israel,
in remembrance of His mercy,

as He spoke to our fathers,
to Abraham and to his descendants forever.
(Luke 1:46–55 MEV)

GERALD CHRISTIAN NORDSKOG
Thanksgiving, 2018

ACKNOWLEDGMENTS

The day the incomparable Dr. Billy Graham passed away, my heart was saddened, but my spirit rejoiced knowing that Dr. Graham has finally received his reward for his faithfulness and determination in evangelizing the saving power of Jesus Christ to the lost world. What an amazing ministry he had!

As thousands of people would walk into the stadium, the resounding music of the great hymns of the church, sung by a mass choir directed by Cliff Barrows, would be heard. The atmosphere was filled with praise proclaiming that "Jesus saves."

My life was so enriched as I grew up playing these anointed hymns on the piano, starting at the age of three. "At the Cross" was the very first hymn I ever played, and to this day I am still blessed by its wonderful lyrics and music.

God strongly impressed on my heart to restore the hymns to our churches and also into the hearts of individuals. Our desire is that you will meditate upon the lyrics and music that were written under the anointing of God's Holy Spirit.

My humble thanks to Jesus for the gift He has given me to be able to share His ministry through music.

Thank you to Jerry and Gail Nordskog, owners of Nordskog Publishing Inc., for going the extra mile in producing and publishing this hymnbook *Hymn Restoration*, a handsome presentation to be treasured in homes and churches everywhere.

Thank you to my darling Cheryl, my wife and life partner. I have seen you spend so many hours in prayer and research in presenting the heart of these composers through Scriptures and devotions. I love the gift of ministry God has given you and I know many will be blessed by it. Cheryl, you have your daddy's heart for ministry.

Thank you to Christina, our daughter, who has researched each hymn to be perfect in notation and clarity for the congregation to sing. Christina and I have collaborated in bringing to you the best hymns for this first volume. I'm proud of you, Christina.

Michelle Shelfer, our editor and consultant, who diligently checked our work to perfection. What an amazing gift God has given you, Michelle. Our family respects and appreciates your work. Thank you, Michelle.

Last, but certainly not least, thank you to my Facebook Family, who have been faithful from the very start of this project. You have been extremely supportive in encouraging me to put these doctrinally correct hymns back into our church pews. Your prayers and support have been the backbone of the *Hymn Restoration* journey.

TABLE OF CONTENTS

INTRODUCTION

We honor today's young musicians and composers and the love and skill they bring to musical worship because we know that the Lord hears their hearts.

Hymn Restoration is about introducing a new generation to the musical treasures of Christian history. We bring to you 101 of the best from the vast wealth of hymns going back centuries. You will immediately recognize the depth of the lyrics and the inspired beauty of the melodies.

Every hymn is presented here alongside a devotion that Cheryl Kartsonakis has written, a chance to think more deeply about the hymns. We are indebted to the wonderful historians of hymnology and their books, some of which date back to the eras in which the hymns were written—historians such as John Julian and Ira Sankey, as well as the modern historians such as Robert Morgan and Kenneth Osbeck. You can refer to them in our Notes section.

We hope that as you encounter these hymns and devotions you will be uplifted and encouraged in your faith. Music is indeed a special language that can touch us with a penetrating poignancy unique among human experiences. *Sing and rejoice!*

Abide with Me

1. A - bide with me: fast falls the e - ven - tide; The dark - ness
2. Swift to its close ebbs out life's lit - tle day; Earth's joys grow
3. I need Thy pres - ence ev - 'ry pass - ing hour: What but Thy

deep - ens: Lord, with me a - bide! When oth - er help - ers
dim, its glo - ries pass a - way; Change and de - cay in
grace can foil the tempt - er's pow'r? Who like Thy - self my

fail, and com - forts flee, Help of the help - less, O a - bide with me!
all a - round I see; O Thou who chang - est not, a - bide with me!
guide and stay can be? Thru cloud and sun - shine, O a - bide with me!

2

Abide with Me

LYRICS BY HENRY FRANCIS LYTE (1793–1847)
MUSIC BY WILLIAM HENRY MONK (1823–1889)

If ye keep My commandments, ye shall abide in My love; even as I have kept My Father's commandments, and abide in His love.
(John 15:10)

Many people are physically sick or even troubled to the point of considering suicide over a loss in their life. The answer for these people is to take refuge in the Lord. If you are sick because of unforgiveness, remember that faith works by love and love always forgives.

Allow Psalm 91 to minister to you, as you say, "I make the Lord my refuge so that no evil or calamity will come into my house, my body, or my mind." By immersion in the Word, which is our daily bread, our minds become like the mind of Christ. Our pastor, Gary McSpadden, teaches that the brain is the physical organ where we store information, and the mind is where we check our spirit and receive thoughts from our guide, God's Holy Spirit.

We have power over the enemy when we read and know God's Word. We also have authority over spirits of evil so we can live victoriously. When we *"resist the devil,"* he will flee from us. You can simply say, "In the powerful Name of Jesus, leave now! I give you no place in my life, my relationships, my finances, or any other area of my life." My dad used to open the door to throw that spirit out! The ugly spirit that whispers, "You can't take this anymore" must flee from the Name of Jesus.

Remember there are no incurable diseases. Just wait on the Lord, spend time with Him in prayer, and read His Word, the Bible, to gain His direction and understanding. Don't wait to fortify; live by faith, for this is the path of a life dedicated to Christ our Lord, pouring into you the revelation of God's Word.

Prayer

Dear God, fill my heart with understanding to accept the light that comes from studying Your Word. Give me an anointing to be able to share this Word with others. Thank You, Lord God.

3

Amen.

All Creatures of Our God and King

All Creatures of Our God and King

LYRICS BY FRANCIS OF ASSISI (1181–1226)

TRANSLATED BY WILLIAM HENRY DRAPER (1855–1933)

MUSIC: GEISTLICHE KIRCHENGESÄNGE (1623), ARR. RALPH VAUGHAN WILLIAMS (1872–1958)

The heavens declare the glory of God;
and the firmament sheweth His handywork.
Day unto day uttereth speech, and night unto night
sheweth knowledge. There is no speech nor language,
where their voice is not heard.
(Psalm 19:1–3)

The lyrics to this hymn were paraphrased by William Henry Draper from St. Francis of Assisi's poem entitled "Canticle of the Sun." It is one of the oldest hymn texts, with St. Francis's lyrics dating back to 1225.

St. Francis of Assisi grew up surrounded by wealth, with the expectation that he would become a merchant like his father. But God had different plans. As a young man, he faced unusual challenges—he was taken prisoner during a border dispute, and upon his release, he suffered an extended illness. A visit to Rome and contact with the beggars there greatly influenced him. St. Francis heard a call from God to renounce his old life and devote himself to a life of poverty and service.

G. K. Chesterton writes about St. Francis and his "Canticle of the Sun," "He sang it wandering in the meadows in the sunnier season of his own career, when he was pouring upwards into the sky all the passions of a poet."[1] The lyrics to this hymn demonstrate St. Francis's love of nature, as they extend a magnificent invitation to all of God's creation—wind, water, sun, fire, and mankind—to join together as one voice in glorious praise of God.

Prayer

Lord, You created each of us and have given us ideas, thoughts, talents, and love of life. May we use all You have given according to Your plan for our lives. Thank You, Lord.

Amen.

All Hail the Power of Jesus' Name

1. All hail the pow'r of Je - sus' Name! Let an - gels pros - trate fall!
2. Ye cho - sen seed of Is - rael's race, Ye ran - somed from the fall,
3. Let ev - 'ry kin - dred, ev - 'ry tribe. On this ter - res - trial ball,
4. O that, with yon - der sa - cred throng, We at His feet may fall!

Bring forth the roy - al di - a - dem, And crown Him Lord of all!
Hail Him who saves you by His grace, And crown Him Lord of all!
To Him all maj - es - ty as - cribe, And crown Him Lord of all!
We'll join the ev - er - last - ing song, And praise Him Lord of all!

They bro't the roy - al di - a - dem, And crown Him Lord of all!
Hail Him who saves you by His grace, And crown Him Lord of all!
To Him all maj - es - ty as - cribe, And crown Him Lord of all!
We'll join the ev - er - last - ing song, And praise Him Lord of all!

6

All Hail the Power of Jesus' Name

<small>LYRICS BY EDWARD PERRONET (1726–1792)
MUSIC BY OLIVER HOLDEN (1765–1844)</small>

*Wherefore God also hath highly exalted Him,
and given Him a name which is above every name:
that at the name of Jesus every knee should bow,
of things in heaven, and things in earth, and things under the earth;
and that every tongue should confess that Jesus Christ is Lord,
to the glory of God the Father.*
(Philippians 2:9–11)

The Reverend Edward Perronet was the son of an Anglican priest. He was a friend of the well-known Wesleys, and also Lady Huntingdon, a philanthropic patroness. Perronet's immortal hymn "**All Hail the Power of Jesus' Name**" has had a tremendous impact on Protestants of all denominations.

The nineteenth-century missionary Reverend E. P. Scott made extraordinary use of "**All Hail the Power of Jesus' Name**" while venturing into the village of a remote inland tribe in India that he wished to evangelize. Suddenly the hostile tribe surrounded him, pointing their spears in a threatening pose. Reverend Scott had nothing in his hands but his violin. So, closing his eyes, he played and sang Perronet's immortal hymn. As he sang he confessed the power of Jesus' Name. Opening his eyes he saw that their spears had dropped and they received him with tears, eagerness, curiosity, and interest. Perronet's hymn won their hearts, enabling Reverend Scott to declare and demonstrate the Gospel message of trusting in the power of Jesus' Name.[2]

Prayer

*Oh God, we eagerly cast our crowns before You, the only One worthy to bear a diadem and crown. You wore the crown of thorns, but now You wear the crown of the King of kings and Lord of lords! We declare with great joy that You are our Sovereign King and Lord, and that Your Name is all powerful. Let us indeed **All Hail the Power of Jesus' Name!***

Amen.

All the Way My Savior Leads Me

1. All the way my Sav-ior leads me; What have I to ask be-side?
2. All the way my Sav-ior leads me; Cheers each wind-ing path I tread,
3. All the way my Sav-ior leads me; O, the full-ness of His love!

Can I doubt His ten-der mer-cy, Who thru life has been my guide?
Gives me grace for ev-'ry tri-al, Feeds me with the liv-ing bread.
Per-fect rest to me is prom-ised In my Fa-ther's house a-bove.

Heav'n-ly peace, di-vin-est com-fort, Here by faith in Him to dwell!
Tho' my wea-ry steps may fal-ter, And my soul a-thirst may be,
When my spir-it, clothed im-mor-tal, Wings its flight to realms of day,

For I know, what-e'er be-fall me, Je-sus do-eth all things well; well.
Gush-ing from the Rock be-fore me, Lo! A spring of joy I see; see.
This my song thru end-less a-ges: Je-sus led me all the way; way.

All the Way My Savior Leads Me

LYRICS BY FANNY J. CROSBY (1820–1915)
MUSIC BY ROBERT LOWRY (1826–1899)

He hath shewed thee, O man, what is good;
and what doth the LORD require of thee, but to do justly,
and to love mercy, and to walk humbly with thy God?
(Micah 6:8)

Did you ever have a need and experience God sending an angel to supply that need?

I once was driving about an hour away to the airport to pick up my husband. I was several miles from the destination when it began to rain. I was in the middle lane of three-lane traffic, with a car on each side, one in front, and one behind me. Suddenly the driver in front of me slammed on his breaks, forcing me to do the same. My car began to spin around to the left. I held the steering wheel tightly, trying to bring the car back to the right to straighten it, but it just kept sliding left. In that instant I cried out, "Jesus, help me stop this car!" By that time my car had completely turned backward, facing the oncoming traffic, but in an instant it seemed to glide on across the road, moving onto the median with the back facing down a muddy embankment—and it stopped! I sat there in perfect peace, giving praise to the Lord Jesus.

A tap at my window caused me to look up, and a man asked me, "Ma'am, are you okay?" I answered, "Yes I am." Then he said, "Lady, that was a total miracle the way you steered that car. It was beautiful! I have never seen anyone drive through cars like that. It was awesome!"

I sat there quietly thinking, *that wasn't me driving*. Yes, it was a miracle. It had to be an angel steering the car through all that traffic, bringing it to safety without touching another car!

There was nothing wrong with my car after this incident, so I drove on to the airport. I was so excited to share with my husband the miracle of God's power and what God had done.

Prayer

*Thank You, Lord God, that there is never a time when You do not hear us. You answer when we call. Lord, we know that Your way is **All the Way My Savior Leads Me**. Thank You, Jesus.*

Amen.

Amazing Grace

1. A - maz - ing grace! how sweet the sound! That
2. 'Twas grace that taught my heart to fear, And
3. Thru man - y dan - gers, toils and snares I
4. When we've been there ten thou - sand years, Bright
5. A - maz - ing grace! how sweet the sound! That

saved a wretch like me! I once was lost, but
grace my fears re - lieved. How pre - cious did that
have al - read - y come. 'Tis grace hath bro't me
shin - ing as the sun, We've no less days to
saved a wretch like me! I once was lost, but

now I'm found; Was blind, but now I see.
grace ap - pear The hour I first be - lieved!
safe thus far, And grace will lead me home.
sing God's praise Than when we'd first be - gun.
now I'm found; Was blind, but now I see.

Amazing Grace

LYRICS BY JOHN NEWTON (1725–1807)
MUSIC: TRADITIONAL FOLK MELODY

To the praise of the glory of His grace, wherein He hath made us accepted in the beloved. In whom we have redemption through His blood, the forgiveness of sins, according to the riches of His grace.
(Ephesians 1:6–7)

John Newton had to give up the innocence of childhood at the very tender age of six. His mother was a frail woman who cherished her son. She taught him to memorize Scripture and also hymns. Her prayer was for his heart to be kept close to God. But when John was not yet seven, his mother died. He was sent to boarding school and began his seafaring career at age eleven with his father. Then the Royal Navy drafted him. When war seemed to be looming on the horizon, John deserted. For this he was captured, beaten, and dismissed from the Navy. John then joined a slave-trading ship's crew, and eventually became a captain, and for six years he carried cargoes of slaves.

In 1754 John read a book entitled *The Imitation of Christ* by Thomas á Kempis. It so impressed him that he left the seaman's life and began studying the Scriptures in Hebrew and Greek. He was ordained in the Church of England and was appointed the curate of Olney in 1764. His mother's prayers were answered.

John Newton, along with his friend, poet William Cowper, produced the famed hymn book known as *The Olney Hymns*, which contained 348 hymns, of which Newton composed 280, including "**Amazing Grace.**"

It was God's **Amazing Grace** that brought a child through the life of a slave trader, to knowledge of the Scriptures and a ministry in the Church.

Prayer

*Thank You, Lord, that we can experience Your **Amazing Grace**, no matter our lives' circumstances. God's **Amazing Grace** will see us through. We praise You for this, in Jesus' Name.*

Amen.

Are You Washed in the Blood?

1. Have you been to Je - sus for the cleans - ing pow'r? Are you washed in the
2. Are you walk - ing dai - ly by the Sav - ior's side? Are you washed in the
3. When the Bride-groom com - eth will your robes be white, pure and white in the
4. Lay a - side the gar - ments that are stained with sin, And be washed in the

blood of the Lamb? Are you ful - ly trust - ing in His grace this hour? Are you
blood of the Lamb? Do you rest each mo - ment in the Cru - ci - fied? Are you
blood of the Lamb? Will your soul be read - y for the man - sions bright, And be
blood of the Lamb; There's a foun - tain flow - ing for the soul un - clean, O be

Chorus

washed in the blood of the Lamb? Are you washed in the blood,
Are you washed in the blood,

In the soul-cleans-ing blood of the Lamb? Are your gar-ments spot-less?
of the Lamb?

Are they white as snow? Are you washed in the blood of the Lamb?

Are You Washed in the Blood?

LYRICS AND MUSIC BY ELISHA ALBRIGHT HOFFMAN (1839–1929)

And the blood of Jesus Christ His Son cleanseth us from all sin.
(1 John 1:7b)

Whoso eateth my flesh, and drinketh my blood
[takes communion], *hath eternal life;*
and I will raise him up at the last day.
(John 6:54)

Have you noticed that in today's Church there seems to be a pattern of avoidance of teaching about the blood of Jesus, shed for our sins? This, in fact, is our precious Gospel, upon which all our hope and joy rests! The deceiving devil is at it again! Let's go directly to the source, God's Word, to find out the truth about the blood of Jesus:

But if we walk in the light, as He is in the light, we have fellowship one with another, and the blood of Jesus Christ His Son cleanseth us from all sin. (1 John 1:7)

And from Jesus Christ, who is the faithful witness, and the first begotten of the dead, and the Prince of the kings of the earth. Unto Him that loved us, and washed us from our sins in His own blood. (Revelation 1:5)

And almost all things are by the law purged with blood; and without shedding of blood is no remission. (Hebrew 9:22)

And I said unto him, Sir, thou knowest. And he said to me, These are they which came out of great tribulation, and have washed their robes, and made them white in the blood of the Lamb. (Revelation 7:14)

Without the shed blood of Jesus there is no forgiveness of sin. One question, my friend: Are you washed in the blood of the Lamb? If not, please pray this prayer:

Prayer

"Jesus, please forgive every sin I have ever committed. Wash me with Your pure blood so that I may be clean. Guide my life from this point on to eternity, in the Name of Jesus. I believe. Amen." Now, find a Bible-believing church that teaches about the shed blood of Jesus.

Amen.

13

At the Cross

1. A - las! and did my Sav - ior bleed? And did my Sov - 'reign die?
2. Was it for crimes that I had done He groaned up - on the tree?
3. Well might the sun in dark - ness hide, And shut His glo - ries in,
4. But drops of grief can ne'er re - pay The debt of love I owe,

Would He de - vote that sa - cred head, For such a worm as I?
A - maz - ing pit - y! grace un - known! And love be - yond de - gree!
When Christ, the might - y Mak - er, died, For man the crea - ture's sin.
Here, Lord, I give my - self a - way; 'Tis all that I can do.

Chorus

At the cross, at the cross, where I first saw the light, And the

bur - den of my heart rolled a - way, rolled a - way,
It was there by faith

I re - ceived my sight, And now I am hap - py all the day.

At the Cross

Lyrics by Isaac Watts (1674–1748)
Music by Ralph Hudson (1843–1901)

Looking unto Jesus the author and finisher of our faith; who for the joy that was set before Him endured the cross, despising the shame, and is set down at the right hand of the throne of God.
(Hebrews 12:2)

Isaac Watts was surely given a supernatural understanding of Jesus as he wrote these lyrics! The lyrics to this wonderful hymn grip my heart as I write this! The second verse says:

Was it for crimes that I had done

He groaned upon the tree?

Amazing pity! Grace unknown!

And love beyond degree!

It was for our sin that Christ Jesus was nailed to the cross. He became submissive to the pain He suffered, so that God would, through Jesus' suffering, forgive you and me. As He hung on the cross on Calvary's hill, His groaning expressed His pity for us, as He observed our lack of understanding of His grace. Indeed, how can mere mortals fathom a love so deep? It surpasses our understanding, unless it is granted to us supernaturally from our Lord Jesus.

We can have knowledge and wisdom far beyond ourselves through the living Word of God, the Bible, but we must encounter and know Jesus as our personal Savior first. Then we can ask Him to give a supernatural revelation for our individual lives! The Word of God, Jesus, became flesh and dwelt among us, but He gives us the opportunity to fellowship with Him in the supernatural as we live obedient to His Word!

Prayer

Father God, give us ears to hear and eyes to see, as Your Word fills us with a desire to be obedient, and the precious Holy Spirit of God comes to be our ever-present teacher when we are saved. Thank You, Jesus, that You were **At the Cross**, *hung there for the remission of our sin. Now You can show us the supernatural power of Your Word.*

Amen.

Be Still, My Soul

Be Still, My Soul

LYRICS BY KATHARINA VON SCHLEGEL (1697–1768)
TRANSLATED BY JANE BORTHWICK (1813–1897)

*Be still, and know that I am God: I will be exalted
among the heathen, I will be exalted in the earth.*
(Psalm 46:10)

ave you ever felt the severe loss when a friend or family member passed unexpectedly? You heart is broken and at that moment you just don't think you will ever be able to overcome the pain you are experiencing.

When my father gave me a call from the hospital one morning, he said, "Hello, my sweet girl. Guess what—the doctor said if I walk completely around this floor of the hospital, I can *go home today*." His voice was somewhat different—there was such joy and excitement that I was thrilled for him. His heart had been skipping beats, but he seemed to be so happy that he was going home. All the family members he lovingly reached out to by phone that morning experienced the joy with him.

About an hour later I received a rather panicky call from my mother. She cried, "Cheryl, Dad is gone!" I was shocked. Calming just a little, she said, "Dad walked around the whole hospital floor. And then, as I turned to set down my bag, I heard him gasp. Then he was gone." Consoling my mother, my mind returned to his excitement as he said to me, "Sweet Girl, today I'm *going home!*" The pain and grief I felt was almost overwhelming, because I had lost my prayer partner and my buddy— my dad.

In the midst of my grief, my heart turned to the love of my Heavenly Father. My precious husband Dino and our girls consoled me, and in those moments God spoke to my heart that Dad had finished his life and had indeed gone home to his peace and rest in the Lord.

Prayer

*Thank You, Father, that through every season in life, You are there. You remove disappointment, grief, and fear, and all sorrow is forgotten when our minds are fixed on You. You restore love and purest joy. Thank You that I can say, "**Be Still, My Soul**," and give over all control to You.*

Amen.

17

Be Thou My Vision

1. Be Thou my Vi - sion, O Lord of my heart;
2. Be Thou my Wis - dom, and Thou my true Word;
3. Be Thou my Breast - plate, my Sword for the fight;
4. Rich - es I heed not, nor man's emp - ty praise;
5. High King of heav - en, Thou heav - en's bright Sun,

be all else but naught to me, save that Thou art;
be Thou ev - er with me, and I with Thee, Lord;
be Thou my whole Ar - mor, be Thou my true Might;
be Thou mine in - her - it - ance, now and al - ways;
O grant me its joys, af - ter vic - t'ry is won;

be Thou my best thought in the day and the night,
be Thou my great Fa - ther, and I Thy true son;
be Thou my soul's Shel - ter, be Thou my strong Tow'r,
be Thou and Thou on - ly the first in my heart,
Great Heart of my own heart, what - ev - er be - fall,

both wak - ing and sleep - ing, Thy pres - ence my light.
be Thou in me dwell - ing, and I with Thee one.
O raise Thou me heav'n - ward, great Pow'r of my pow'r.
O High King of heav - en, my Treas - ure Thou art,
still be Thou my vi - sion, O Rul - er of all.

Be Thou My Vision

TRADITIONAL IRISH HYMN
TRANSLATED BY MARY ELIZABETH BYRNE (1880–1931)

And when they found not His body, they came, saying,
that they had also seen a vision of angels, which said that He was
alive. And certain of them which were with us went to the sepulchre,
and found it even so as the women had said:
but Him they saw not.
(Luke 24:23–24)

As we read further in Luke 24, Jesus says to the two with whom He is traveling on the road to Emmaus, "*O fools, and slow of heart to believe all that the prophets have spoken: Ought not Christ to have suffered these things, and to enter into His glory?*" (vv. 25–26) Their vision is impaired. They can't see who is speaking to them, nor understand His purposes. He teaches the two about Himself, as written in the Scriptures of Moses and all the prophets. As they draw near to their village, Jesus acts as though He is going to travel further on. But the two implore Him to stay with them because it is almost evening, and He does so.

As Jesus sits at a meal with his travel companions, He takes the bread, blesses, and breaks it, and gives it to them. Suddenly, their eyes are opened such that they know Him—and He vanishes right out of their sight.

With the eyes of their understanding enlightened, these two ask one another, "*Did not our heart burn within us, while He talked with us by the way, and while He opened to us the Scriptures?*" (v. 32)

Just as Jesus is able to open the eyes of these two disciples' understanding, and that of all the disciples in Jerusalem, so He can open the eyes of your understanding as well. Invite Jesus to "**Be Thou My Vision,**" so that you may see Him clearly and understand the extraordinary work He has done on our behalf!

Prayer

Father, as we read Your Word, may we learn how we too may praise and bless You, our God, with our whole heart! In the miraculous Name of Jesus.

Amen.

Beneath the Cross of Jesus

1. Be - neath the cross of Je - sus I fain would take my stand,
2. Up - on that cross of Je - sus Mine eye at times can see
3. I take, O cross, thy shad - ow For my a - bid - ing place;

The shad - ow of a might - y rock With - in a wea - ry land;
The ver - y dy - ing form of One Who suf - fered there for me;
I ask no oth - er sun - shine than The sun - shine of His face;

A home with - in the wil - der - ness, A rest up - on the way,
And from my smit - ten heart, with tears, Two won - ders I con - fess,—
Con - tent to let the world go by, To know no gain or loss,

From the burn - ing of the noon - tide heat, And the bur - den of the day.
The won - ders of His glo - ri - ous love, And my own worth - less - ness.
My sin - ful self my on - ly shame, My glo - ry all the cross.

Beneath the Cross of Jesus

LYRICS BY ELIZABETH CLEPHANE (1830–1869)
MUSIC BY FREDERICK C. MAKER (1844–1927)

And a man shall be as an hiding place from the wind, and a covert from the tempest; as rivers of water in a dry place, as the shadow of a great rock in a weary land. (Isaiah 32:2)

To whom He said, This is the rest wherewith ye may cause the weary to rest; and this is the refreshing. (Isaiah 28:12a)

And there shall be a tabernacle for a shadow in the daytime from the heat, and for a place of refuge, and for a covert from storm and from rain. (Isaiah 4:6)

For My yoke is easy, and My burden is light. (Matthew 11:30)

"Beneath the Cross of Jesus" was written by Elizabeth Clephane in 1868, one year before her death. She lived most of her life in or near Melrose, Scotland. Her father was the county sheriff. She was a very cheerful person who focused on what she could do for others. Her friends called her "Sunbeam."

In the *Family Treasury* we read of Clephane's hymns, "Written on the very edge of this life, with the better land fully in the view of faith, they seem to us footsteps printed on the sands of Time, where these sands touch the ocean of Eternity."[3]

Elizabeth loved poetry and wrote several hymns—one you may know is "The Ninety and Nine," about the shepherd who left his sheep to find that one lost sheep, a story told in Matthew 18:12–14. Just think of what our Savior suffered so that we would not have to. We may freely receive the gift of salvation and eternal life. What grace He has bestowed on us! If you don't have Jesus in your heart and life as your Savior, just ask Him into your heart now and He will forgive your sin. Pray this:

Prayer

Lord Jesus, come into my heart, forgive me of my sins and make me whole. I believe in You, Jesus, and ask You from this time forward to direct my life. Teach me through the Holy Spirit how to live a Christian life. I love You, and I thank You for the wonderful gift of eternal life. Amen.

Blessed Assurance

1. Bless-ed as - sur - ance, Je - sus is mine! O what a fore - taste of
2. Per - fect sub - mis - sion, per - fect de - light, Vi - sions of rap - ture now
3. Perf - ect sub - mis - sion, all is at rest; I in my Sav - ior am

glo - ry di - vine! Heir of sal - va - tion, pur - chase of God,
burst on my sight; An - gels de - scend - ing bring from a - bove
hap - py and blest; Watch - ing and wait - ing, look - ing a - bove,

Chorus

Born of His Spir - it, washed in His blood.
Ech - oes of mer - cy, whis - pers of love. This is my sto - ry, this is my song,
Filled with His good - ness, lost in His love.

Prais - ing my Sav - ior all the day long; This is my sto - ry,

this is my song, Prais - ing my Sav - ior all the day long.

Blessed Assurance

LYRICS BY FANNY J. CROSBY (1820–1915)
MUSIC BY PHOEBE P. KNAPP (1839–1908)

> *That their hearts might be comforted, being knit together in love,
> and unto all riches of the full assurance of understanding, to the
> acknowledgement of the mystery of God, and of the Father, and of
> Christ; In whom are hid all the treasures of wisdom and knowledge.*
> (Colossians 2:2–3)

Fanny J. Crosby shares in her autobiography about the process of composing what she calls "hymn-poems."

In a successful song words and music must harmonize, not only in number of syllables, but in subject matter and especially accent. In nine cases out of ten the success of a hymn depends directly upon these qualities. Thus, melodies tell their own tale, and it is the purpose of the poet to interpret this musical story into language.... "Blessed Assurance" was written to a melody composed by my friend, Mrs. Joseph F. Knapp [Phoebe Knapp]; she played it over once or twice on the piano and then asked me what it said to me. I replied,

Blessed assurance, Jesus is mine...[4]

We learn of an interesting event in which Fanny was honored for this hymn at an occasion when D. L. Moody was preaching:

This day the church was so crowded she could find nowhere to sit. Moody's son, Will, seeing her, offered to find her a seat. To her bewilderment, he led her onto the platform just as the crowd was singing "Blessed Assurance." Moody, Sr., jumped to his feet, raised his hand, and interrupted the singing. "Praise the Lord!" he shouted. "Here comes the authoress!"

Fanny took her seat amid thunderous ovation, humbly thanking God for making her a blessing to so many.[5]

Prayer

*Thank You, Lord, for women of God who will use their time and talents to bless the lives of others, with the **Blessed Assurance** that many will be saved.*

Amen.

Break Thou the Bread of Life

1. Break Thou the bread of life, Dear Lord, to me, As Thou didst
2. Bless Thou the truth, dear Lord, to me, to me, As Thou didst
3. Thou art the bread of life, O Lord, to me, Thy ho - ly

break the loaves Be - side the sea; Be - yond the sa - cred page,
bless the bread by Gal - i - lee; Then shall all bond - age cease,
Word the truth That sav - eth me; Give me to eat and live

I seek Thee, Lord; My spir - it pants for Thee, O liv - ing Word!
All fet - ters fall; And I shall find my peace, my All in All.
With Thee a - bove; Teach me to love Thy truth, For Thou art love.

Break Thou the Bread of Life

LYRICS BY MARY ANN LATHBURY (1841–1913)
MUSIC BY WILLIAM F. SHERWIN (1826–1888)

For the bread of God is He which cometh down from heaven, and giveth life unto the world. Then said they unto Him, Lord, evermore give us this bread. And Jesus said unto them, I am the bread of life: he that cometh to Me shall never hunger; and he that believeth on Me shall never thirst.
(John 6:33–35)

I remember as a child being taught that a small boy once went to hear the Lord teach and brought with him five loaves and two fishes. What a blessed trust in the Lord it took for the unselfish child to give to the Master all that he had! We too are asked by our Savior to give our all to Him, so that Jesus can perform a supernatural miracle in our natural lives.

We are to give ten percent of our income to supply the ministry of the Lord with what is needed. You know, that is obedience to God. This is a command, but whether or not to be obedient is our choice. When we use God's ten percent we are taking what belongs to God. We have ninety percent to use for ourselves.

If we have a problem with giving we need to check our hearts! The Bible, God's Word, says in Luke 6:38, *"Give, and it shall be given unto you; good measure, pressed down, and shaken together, and running over, shall men give into your bosom. For with the same measure that ye mete withall it shall be measured to you again."* So it is with your generosity in giving gifts to God the Father, through the church and to His children. Luke 6:36–37 says, *"Be ye therefore merciful, as your Father also is merciful. Judge not, and ye shall not be judged: condemn not, and ye shall not be condemned: forgive, and ye shall be forgiven."*

So **Break Thou the Bread of Life** and give to others—as it is up to you to make a choice to give—and our God will surely lavish you with His love and grace!

Prayer

Thank You, Lord God, for teaching us to be givers. May we have ears to hear and eyes to see Your miraculous displays of love toward us.

Amen.

A Child of the King

A Child of the King

LYRICS BY HARRIET E. BUELL (1834–1910)
MUSIC BY JOHN B. SUMNER (1838–1913)

*Which in His times He shall shew, who is the blessed
and only Potentate, the King of kings, and Lord of lords.*
(1 Timothy 6:15)

This song is so special and precious to me because my own mother sang it. Helen McCann began preaching at age twelve after her salvation experience in an arbor revival. When she was nineteen she married my father, Reverend Boyd McSpadden, and they pastored together. Mother was quite dramatic in her presentations, so as a young child this message impacted my heart deeply. Now I sing, as she did, dramatizing this song to fully communicate its wonderful message. Harriet Buell wrote these lyrics one Sunday as she was returning home from church.

The Lord has a strong place of victory for each of us, if we listen and pay attention. He says, "I will show you; I have the plan for you; I will place you in a strong place of victory!" Please—do not make plans based on politicians or what the media says. Keep your eyes on God's Word, and follow His plan. He loves you so much, so be clean in your mind and live far from covetousness.

"*For the love of money is the root of all evil*" (1 Timothy 6:10). When we walk in the favor of our Lord we are resting in "our wealthy place." However, the key to this kind of blessing is total obedience to God and His Word.

When we observe the lyrics of this song by Harriet Buell, we see that "My Father is rich," and "I'm a child of the King." "My Father's own Son" is "the Savior of men [people]." "They're building a palace for me over there! Though here I'm a stranger, yet still I may sing: All glory to God, I'm a child of the King!"

Prayer

Oh, dear Father, Thank You for Your saving power, and that You adopt all who are willing to follow You! We become Your children of light in this world, reflecting Your power. Thank You for the riches of Your grace, for they are eternal riches. We praise You, our Lord.

Amen.

No. 14

Come Thou Fount of Every Blessing

1. Come, Thou Fount of ev-'ry bless-ing, Tune my heart to sing Thy grace;
2. Here I raise my Eb - e - ne - zer: Hith - er by Thy help I've come!
3. O to grace how great a debt - or Dai - ly I'm con - strained to be!

Streams of mer - cy, nev - er ceas - ing, Call for songs of loud - est praise.
And I hope by Thy good pleas - ure Safe - ly to ar - rive at home.
Let Thy good - ness like a fet - ter Bind my wan - d'ring heart to Thee.

Teach me some me - lo - dious son - net, Sung by flam - ing tongues a - bove;
Je - sus sought me when a stran - ger, Wan - d'ring from the fold of God;
Proned to wan - der, Lord I feel it, Prone to leave the God I love;

Praise the mount! I'm fixed up - on it, Mount of Thy re - deem - ing love.
He to res - cue me from dan - ger In - ter - posed His pre - cious blood.
Here's my heart, O take and seal it, Seal it for Thy courts a - bove.

Come Thou Fount of Every Blessing

LYRICS BY ROBERT ROBINSON (1735–1790)
MUSIC FROM WYETH'S *REPOSITORY OF SACRED MUSIC*

> *But when he* [John the Baptist] *saw many of the Pharisees and Sadducees come to his baptism, he said unto them, O generation of vipers, who hath warned you to flee from the wrath to come? Bring forth therefore fruits meet for repentance.*
> (Matthew 3:7–8)

At the death of his father, Robert Robinson had to go to work as a young boy. Without a father's guidance, Robert fell in with bad companions. One day his gang of rowdies harassed a drunken Gypsy and bribed her with liquor to tell their fortune. She pointed her finger at Robert and told him that he would live to see his children and grandchildren. This struck deep into Robert's heart and caused him to consider his future.

Robert went to hear the great preacher George Whitfield, whose text happened to be from Matthew 3:7 (above). "*O generation of vipers, who hath warned you to flee from the wrath to come?*" Robert left there with a deep sense of his own sinfulness that troubled him for years. Finally, three years later at the age of twenty, he made peace with God.

Robert became a Methodist preacher, and in 1757 he wrote this hymn expressing his joy in his new faith. In the hymn is this stanza:

> *Prone to wander, Lord, I feel it, Prone to leave the God I love.*
> *Here's my heart, O take and seal it. Seal it for Thy courts above.*

Robert Robinson was indeed prone to wander, as he left the Methodists and became a Baptist, and later left the Baptists and became a Unitarian. In Julian we read, "His three changes of ecclesiastical relationship show that he was somewhat unstable and impulsive."[6] We are admonished in the Bible to check all teachings against the Word of God.

Prayer

Father God, Lord Jesus our Savior, and precious Holy Spirit, we know that Your Word, the unfailing Word of God—the Bible—is true. We also know that the words You spoke to the men of God who wrote the texts of the Bible were perfect. Jesus, You are the Living Word of God. You came to earth to give us salvation and we praise and thank You.

Amen.

29

Esther Accuses Haman, 1866 (Gustave Doré)

Count Your Blessings

LYRICS BY JOHNSON OATMAN JR. (1856–1922)
MUSIC BY EDWIN O. EXCELL (1851–1921)

For which of you, intending to build a tower, sitteth not down first, and counteth the cost, whether he have sufficient to finish it? Lest haply, after he hath laid the foundation, and is not able to finish it, all that behold it begin to mock him.
(Luke 14:28–29)

The story told in the book of Esther demonstrates how those acting contrary to the will of God sometimes fall into traps of their own making. Mordecai raised beautiful Esther as his own daughter. Esther finds favor with King Ahasuerus of Persia and is crowned his new queen, yet she hides her Jewish heritage from him. Mordecai seeks the well-being of the king, and saves him from an assassination plot, communicating through Esther the queen.

After these things, King Ahasuerus advances a man named Haman to a position above all the princes. When Mordecai refuses to bow to Haman, Haman is enraged. He deceptively obtains a decree from the king to kill all the Jews in Persia because of his hatred for Mordecai, the Jew. Haman builds a huge gallows on which to hang Mordecai, but because of the brave intervention of Esther, who risks her life to preserve her people, the Jews are saved, Mordecai is advanced by the king, and Haman himself hangs on the gallows he built for Mordecai.

Watch out for the trap you set for others; it may turn out to be your own! Galatians 6:7–8 tells us, *"Be not deceived; God is not mocked: for whatsoever a man soweth, that shall he also reap. For he that soweth to his flesh shall of the flesh reap corruption; but he that soweth to the Spirit shall of the Spirit reap life everlasting."*

Instead of seeking the harm of others, be a blessing to others, and **Count Your Blessings,** because "God is over all."

Prayer

Lord, give us faith in You when we're disappointed in others, that we may never retort but pray for our enemies and do good to them so that they may become children of the King. Thank You, Lord.

Amen.

Count Your Blessings

1. When up-on life's bil-lows you are tem - pest - tossed,
2. Are you ev - er bur-dened with a load of care?
3. So, a-mid the con-flict, wheth-er great or small,

(1. When up-on life's bil-lows you are tem-pest-tossed,

When you are dis-cour-aged, think - ing all is lost,
Does the cross seem heav-y you are called to bear?
Do not be dis-cour-aged, God is o - ver all;

When you are dis-cour-aged, think - ing all is lost,

Count your man - y bless - ings, name them one by one,
Count your man - y bless - ings, ev - 'ry doubt will fly,
Count your man - y bless - ings, an - gels will at - tend,

Count your man - y bless - ings, name them one by one,

And it will sur - prise you what the Lord hath done.
And you will be sing - ing as the days go by.
Help and com - fort give you to your jour - ney's end.

And it will sur - prise you what the Lord hath done.)

Count Your Blessings, *continued*

Chorus

Count your blessings, name them one by one;
Count your many blessings, name them one by one;

Count your blessings, see what God hath done;
Count your many blessings, see what God hath done;

Rit...

Count your blessings, name them one by one;
Count your many blessings,

a tempo

Count your many blessings, see what God hath done.

Crown Him with Many Crowns

1. Crown Him with man-y crowns, The Lamb up-on the throne;
2. Crown Him the Lord of life, Who tri-umphed o'er the grave,
3. Crown Him the Lord of peace, Whose pow'r a scep-ter sways
4. Crown Him the Lord of heav'n, One with the Fa-ther known,

Hark, how the heav-n'ly an-them drowns All mu-sic but its own!
Who rose vic-to-rious in the strife For those He came to save!
From pole to pole, that wars may cease, Ab-sorbed in prayer and praise:
And the blest Spir-it, thru Him giv'n From yon-der glor-ious throne!

A-wake, my soul, and sing Of Him who died for thee,
His glo-ries now we sing, Who died, and rose on high,
His reign shall know no end, And round His pierc-ed feet
All hail, Re-de-emer hail! For Thou has died for me;

And hail Him as thy match-less King Thru all e-ter-ni-ty.
Who died e-te-rnal life to bring, And lives that death may die.
Fair flow'rs of Par-a-dise ex-tend, Their fra-grance ev-er sweet.
Thy praise and glo-ry shall not fail Thru-out e-ter-ni-ty.

Crown Him with Many Crowns

LYRICS BY MATTHEW BRIDGES (1800–1894)
MUSIC BY GEORGE J. ELVEY (1816–1893)

And when they had platted a crown of thorns, they put it upon His head, and a reed in His right hand: and they bowed the knee before Him, and mocked Him, saying, Hail, King of the Jews! And they spit upon Him, and took the reed, and smote Him on the head.
(Matthew 27:29–30)

In the first stanza of this song, we sing, "**Crown Him** with many crowns, the Lamb upon the throne." Our magnificent Savior, the King of kings, gave His life unto a death of pain and sorrow. He did this so we would each awaken—that is, come from our human brain with its thoughts of self alone and become aware of this whole new realm of the Spirit of God that awaits us.

Hymn writer Matthew Bridges wrote about Jesus as our "matchless King." No other could have loved us so much, and not only in this life will we praise, or "hail," Him, but we will praise Him forever and ever in the life we will live with Him throughout eternity.

Stanza two speaks of crowning Him "the Lord of life," because He died this cruel death upon the cross, but on the third day He "rose victorious," for Jesus Christ overcomes death!

In stanza three we sing, "**Crown Him** the Lord of peace," for He gave His life to restore peace to our broken relationship with Him. In spite of our rebellion and the strife that resulted, we are given God's peace.

Stanza four reads, "**Crown Him** the Lord of heaven," for He left His perfect throne to rescue us from the grave. "Hail, Redeemer," *praise Him, praise Him, praise Him! Thy praise shall never, ever fail throughout eternity.* **Crown Him with Many Crowns**, for He is worthy!

Prayer

Oh Lord, we know that You are worthy and miraculous. We thank You, Lord our God, and know we can never praise You enough for Your sacrifice in coming to earth to suffer and die, but also in rising victoriously to sit at God's right hand. Praise Your matchless Name!

Amen.

Day by Day

Day by Day

LYRICS BY CAROLINA SANDELL-BERG (1832–1903)
TRANSLATED BY A. L. SKOOG (1854–1934)
MUSIC BY OSCAR AHNFELT (1813–1882)

Boast not thyself of to morrow; for thou knowest not what a day may bring forth.
(Proverbs 27:1)

Carolina Sandell was the child of a Lutheran pastor in Fröderyd, Sweden. As a child, instead of playing with her peers, she preferred to play quietly in her father's study while he worked.

Lina began hymn writing when she was young. Then, on an occasion when she accompanied her father on a boat journey, an unexpected tragedy occurred. As the boat gave a sudden jolt, her father was thrown overboard, and Lina helplessly watched her father drown before anyone could come to his assistance. She was twenty-six years of age.

Lina poured her grief into her music at that time, and the fourteen songs from her twenty-sixth year of life gripped the hearts of those who heard them.

Lina was thought of as the Swedish Fanny Crosby. "**Day by Day**" was set to music, like many of her lyrics, by Oscar Ahnfelt, about whom Lina once said, "Ahnfelt has sung my songs into the hearts of the people."[7]

"**Day by Day**" offers comfort to people in their times of need, with its words of "peace and rest" and assurance of God's consoling presence through our trials.

Prayer

Jesus, thank You for sweet songs of peace, mercy, love, strength, and power to overcome times in life when we only can turn to You for the answers. Thank You, Jesus.

Amen.

Fairest Lord Jesus

1. Fair - est Lord Je - sus! Ru - ler of all na - ture!
2. Fair are the mead - ows, Fair - er still the wood - lands,
3. Fair is the sun - shine, Fair - er still the moon - light,

O Thou of God and man the Son!
Robed in the bloom - ing garb of spring;
And all the twin - kling star - ry host;

Thee will I cher - ish, Thee will I hon - or,
Je - sus is fair - er, Je - sus is pur - er,
Je - sus shines bright - er, Je - sus shines pur - er,

Thou, my soul's glo - ry, joy, and crown.
Who makes the woe - ful heart to sing.
Than all the an - gels heav'n can boast.

Fairest Lord Jesus

LYRICS AUTHOR UNKNOWN

TRANSLATED BY JOSEPH AUGUST SEISS (1823–1904)

MUSIC: "CRUSADER'S HYMN" (UNCERTAIN ORIGIN)

For unto us a child is born, unto us a Son is given…and His name shall be called Wonderful, Counsellor, The mighty God, The everlasting Father, The Prince of Peace.

(Isaiah 9:6)

"**F**airest Lord Jesus" first appeared in 1677 in a Jesuit hymnbook entitled *Münster Gesangbuch*. However, the text existed fifteen years earlier in a manuscript dated 1662. It was from Roman Catholic Jesuits in Germany. This hymn is shrouded in mystery, for no human took credit for writing the verses. It appeared in a Lutheran Sunday school book in 1873.

If you surround yourself with things that are beautiful to you, they will inspire and encourage you and make you creative. What you choose to think on will be either life or death to you. Discipline your thought life by either welcoming a thought or refusing it. When God thinks of you, He wants to prosper you and give you good health, favor, and joy. God's plan for you is success—a plan for wholeness, nothing missing, nothing broken. Jeremiah 29:11 says,

For I know the thoughts that I think toward you, saith the LORD, thoughts of peace, and not of evil, to give you an expected end.

You can apply this to every area of your life: your marriage, your career, your health, your finances, your journey! God has a plan for each of our lives. If we find what is planned for us by the Lord, our success could be endless!

Prayer

*Our dear **Fairest Lord Jesus**, please apply Your plan to each of our lives so that we will have a wonderful life of bringing others to heaven with us. Your spirit is so lovely; help us to become more like You each day.*

Amen.

For the Beauty of the Earth

1. For the beau - ty of the earth, For the glo - ry of the skies,
2. For the beau - ty of each hour Of the day and of the night,
3. For Thy church that ev - er - more Lift - eth ho - ly hands a - bove,

For the love which from our birth O - ver and a - round us lies,
Hill and vale, and tree, and flow'r, Sun and moon, and stars of light:
Of - f'ring up on ev - 'ry shore Her pure sac - ri - fice of love,

Chorus

Lord of all, to Thee we raise This our hymn of grate - ful praise.

Hymn to the Flowers, 1874

40

For the Beauty of the Earth

Lyrics by Folliott Sandford Pierpoint (1835–1917)
Music by Conrad Kocher (1786–1872)

He hath made every thing beautiful in his time: also He hath set the world in their heart, so that no man can find out the work that God maketh from the beginning to the end.
(Ecclesiastes 3:11)

When we read of how God created the heavens and the earth, we learn that He spoke them into existence. When we speak our words, we also create our world filled with mental images that can affect ourselves or other people. Emotions can sometimes cause us to act on what was said, for either good or bad. But when we look to the Bible or to prayer for any situation, we hear and are directed by the Holy Spirit of God.

When God made the Garden of Eden, He created such beauty, but God Himself was still not done! So, God made a man and fellowshipped together with him in the garden. Adam liked the birds, the fish, and the animals, and He loved his Father God, but God still felt Adam needed a mate in order to be complete. He caused Adam to fall asleep, then took a rib from Adam's side and made a woman called Eve. God then told them to be fruitful.

When we are speaking to someone, we need to think about what we are creating or tearing down. Are we creating joy or sadness? Do we create peace, or are we just busy talkers? Sometimes we are loud and just want our words to stir up a situation or make people notice us. When we talk to God, He wants to hear love, thanks, and appreciation before we ask for anything. **For the Beauty of the Earth**, let your mind think—before you speak. Don't you think God had a perfect plan before He spoke the world into place? Please take time and just think about it!

Prayer

Lord, we know You give all of us creative thoughts and words. Let us know how to use this creativity to glorify Your Kingdom and create beauty in other people's lives.

Amen.

Give Me Thy Heart

1. "Give Me thy heart," says the Fa-ther a-bove, No gift so pre-cious to
2. "Give Me thy heart," says the Sav-ior of men, Call-ing in mer-cy a-
3. "Give Me thy heart," says the Spir-it di-vine, "All that thou hast, to My

Him as our love, Soft-ly He whis-pers wher-ev-er thou art,
gain and a-gain; "Turn now from sin, and from e-vil de-part,
keep-ing re-sign; Grace more a-bound-ing is Mine to im-part,

Chorus

"Grate-ful-ly trust Me, and give Me thy heart."
Have I not died for thee? Give Me thy heart." "Give Me thy heart,
Make full sur-ren-der and give Me thy heart."

p

Give me thy heart," Hear the soft whis-per, wher-ev-er thou art; From this dark

world, He would draw thee a-part, Speak-ing so ten-der-ly, "Give Me thy heart."

Give Me Thy Heart

Lyrics by Eliza E. Hewitt (1851–1920)
Music by William J. Kirkpatrick (1838–1921)

My son, give me thine heart, and let thine eyes observe my ways.
(Proverbs 23:26)

*But without faith it is impossible to please Him: for he that cometh
to God must believe that He is, and that He is a rewarder
of them that diligently seek Him.*
(Hebrews 11:6)

In Jeremiah 17:9 it says, "*The heart is deceitful above all things, and desperately wicked: who can know it?*" Oh, how God wants to give us a new, clean heart!

As we know, the only way to receive a clean heart is by our salvation experience. This was made possible when Jesus went to the cross to die, and He shed His cleansing blood so we could have a cleansed and renewed heart. The only thing needed from you is to say: "Jesus, I have sinned, and I ask in Your powerful Name, Jesus, please come into my heart now. Please forgive every sin I have ever committed against You, Lord, or any other person. I thank You, for I have faith to believe I am forgiven. My sin is gone and I am free from the burden of it. From now on, Lord, You will never remember my sins again. Amen." This *amen* means "so be it!"

You too need never remember any sin that was in your past. When you invite Jesus into your heart, you get a new "DNA," a blood transfusion and a supernatural washing away of sin.

When you ask the Lord to save you, He does! Right then He places the Holy Spirit inside of you, for guidance and angels of protection all around you.

"*He that abideth in me, and I in him, the same bringeth forth much fruit*" (John 15:5). Jesus just asks of you, "**Give Me Thy Heart.**"

Prayer

Lord Jesus, each day as we awaken, may we take time to give You our heart before we do any other thing. Thank You, Lord.

43

Glory to His Name (Down at the Cross)

1. Down at the cross where my Sav - ior died, Down where from cleans-ing from
2. I am so won - drous - ly saved from sin, Je - sus so sweet - ly a -
3. O pre - cious foun - tain that saves from sin, I am so glad I have

sin I cried, There to my heart was the blood ap - plied; Glo - ry to His Name.
bides with - in, There at the cross where He took me in; Glo - ry to His Name.
en - tered in; There Je - sus saves me and keeps me clean; Glo - ry to His Name.

Chorus

Glo - ry to His Name, Glo - ry to His Name;

There to my heart was the blood ap - plied; Glo - ry to His Name.

Glory to His Name (Down at the Cross)

Lyrics by Elisha A. Hoffman (1839–1929)
Music by John H. Stockton (1813–1877)

Give unto the Lord the glory due unto His name;
worship the Lord in the beauty of holiness.
(Psalm 29:2)

That we should be to the praise of His glory,
who first trusted in Christ.
(Ephesians 1:12)

We read about John Stockton in Nutter's 1911 publication, *The Hymns and Hymn Writers of the Church*, that he was:

…a Methodist minister, was born in 1813, and died in 1877. He was a member of the New Jersey Annual Conference of the Methodist Episcopal Church.… He was not only a preacher, but a musician and composer of tunes, as well as a hymn writer. He published two gospel song books: *Salvation Melodies*, 1874, and *Precious Songs*, 1875.[8]

After attending a service one Sunday at Arch Street Church in Philadelphia, Stockton passed away very suddenly.

We must be ready each day to meet Jesus. If we are cleansed— washed in the blood of the Lamb—we will be caught up to meet Him, just after the dead in Christ shall rise. In the twinkling of an eye we will rise to meet Him in the air and forever be with Him—our Lord! **Glory to His Name!**

Prayer

Oh Lord, You are our Lord and Master. Thank You for allowing us to be Your blessed children. Please use our lives to glorify You in the Kingdom of God.

Amen.

God of Our Fathers

1. God of our fathers, whose al - might - y hand
2. Thy love di - vine hath led us in the past;
3. From war's a - larms, from dead - ly, pest - i - lence,
4. Re - fresh Thy peo - ple on their toil - some way;

Leads forth in beau - ty all the star - ry band
In this free land by Thee our lot is cast;
Be Thy strong arm our ev - er sure de - fense;
Lead us from night to nev - er - end - ing day;

Of shin - ning worlds in splen - dor thru the skies,
Be Thou our rul - er, guar - dian, guide and stay,
Thy true re - li - gion in our hearts in - crease,
Fill all our lives with love and grace di - vine,

Our grate - ful songs be - fore Thy throne a - rise. A - men.
Thy Word our law, Thy path our cho - sen way.
Thy boun - teous good - ness nour - ish us in peace.
And glo - ry, laud and praise be ev - er thine.

God of Our Fathers

LYRICS BY DANIEL CRANE ROBERTS (1841–1907)
MUSIC BY GEORGE WILLIAM WARREN (1828–1902)

As every man hath received the gift, even so minister the same one to another, as good stewards of the manifold grace of God.
(1 Peter 4:10)

The blessings we receive from God are not only for our benefit but also for the benefit of others. We are blessed so that we may be a blessing. In our words and deeds to others we use our giftings. Our lives benefit from serving others, primarily those in need who cannot help themselves. When we reach out to help, we gather friendships. Friendships are wealth! Our greatest wealth is not measured in currency or riches but in the relationships we make throughout our lives.

"**God of Our Fathers**" by Daniel Crane Roberts was sung for the first time on July 4th, 1876, at a church in Brandon, Vermont. Roberts wrote the hymn for the first Centennial Celebration of the United States of America.

George W. Warren composed the music to this wonderful hymn. Warren was at the top of his profession as an organist, although he had no formal training. He graduated from Racine College in Wisconsin and afterward held many positions as organist, including St. Peter's Episcopal and St. Paul's in Albany, New York, and Holy Trinity Church in Brooklyn. While at St. Thomas' Church in New York he composed anthems and service music and edited *Hymns and Tunes as Sung at St. Thomas' Church* in 1888. When Warren passed away, no music was performed at his funeral—attended by many thousands of admirers—because it was believed that no one could play as well as George William Warren.

Prayer

Father God, may we hear Your voice and use our talents to the fullest extent, knowing that if we give all glory to You and take none for ourselves, You will lift us to heights we could not have thought possible while bringing others to You. Thank You, Lord, for Your goodness to us.

Amen.

Grace Greater Than Our Sin

1. Mar - vel - ous grace of our lov - ing Lord, Grace that ex - ceeds our sin and our guilt,
2. Dark is the stain that we can - not hide, What can a - vail to wash it a - way?
3. Mar - vel - ous, in - fi - nite, match-less grace, Free - ly bes-towed on all who be - lieve;

Yond - er on Cal - va-ry's mount out -poured, There where the blood of the Lamb was shed.
Look! there is flow-ing a crim - son tide: Whit - er than snow you may be to - day.
You that are long-ing to see His face, Will you this mo-ment His grace re -ceive?

Chorus

Grace, grace, God's grace, Grace that will par-don and cleanse with - in;
Mar - vel - ous grace, in - fin - ite grace,

Grace, grace, God's grace. Grace that is great-er than all our sin.
Mar - vel - ous grace, in - fin - ite grace,

Grace Greater Than Our Sin

Lyrics by Julia H. Johnston (1849–1919)

Music by Daniel B. Towner (1850–1919)

But where sin abounded, grace did much more abound.
(Romans 5:20b)

There is absolutely no question as to where the Bible stands on abortion. This is because Jesus, the Savior and Lord, said that He came to give us life, abundant life. *"And be not conformed to this world: but be ye transformed by the renewing of your mind, that ye may prove what is that good, and acceptable, and perfect, will of God"* (Romans 12:2).

Let's look at this Scripture more closely. It says not to allow yourself to be squeezed into the forms of this world. If you live like the world you will be overcome by the world's ideas, ideals, actions, and ways! Instead, you can be transformed by the renewal of your mind through God's Word.

Please don't let satan, the world's deceiver, the god of this world, deceive you into this world's idea that you have the "right to choose" to destroy a life that Almighty God has given to you to love and cherish. God says NO; renew your mind with what God calls *"the Word of life"* (1 John 1:1)!

What a wonderful hymn Julia H. Johnston has written. God's grace is simple, yet so profound! God's unfathomable forgiveness and love are found in His **Grace Greater Than Our Sin**. *"We have access by faith into this grace wherein we stand, and rejoice in hope of the glory of God"* (Romans 5:2).

*Dear Father, thank You that the Word became flesh. Our Jesus came to this earth, and dwelt amongst us, giving His life in exchange for our salvation. Please transform us by Your **Grace Greater Than Our Sin**!*

Hallelujah, What a Savior!

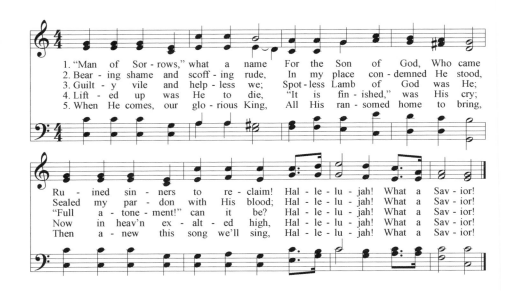

1. "Man of Sor - rows," what a name For the Son of God, Who came
2. Bear - ing shame and scoff - ing rude, In my place con - demned He stood,
3. Guilt - y vile and help - less we; Spot - less Lamb of God was He;
4. Lift - ed up was He to die, "It is fin - ished," was His cry;
5. When He comes, our glo - rious King, All His ran - somed home to bring,

Ru - ined sin - ners to re - claim! Hal - le - lu - jah! What a Sav - ior!
Sealed my par - don with His blood; Hal - le - lu - jah! What a Sav - ior!
"Full a - tone - ment!" can it be? Hal - le - lu - jah! What a Sav - ior!
Now in heav'n ex - alt - ed high, Hal - le - lu - jah! What a Sav - ior!
Then a - new this song we'll sing, Hal - le - lu - jah! What a Sav - ior!

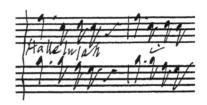

Händel's Hallelujah Autograph, 1741

Hallelujah, What a Savior!

LYRICS AND MUSIC BY PHILIP P. BLISS (1838–1876)

To the only wise God our Saviour, be glory and majesty,
dominion and power, both now and ever. Amen.
(Jude 1:25)

Change is the only constant in life. Dr. A. R. Bernard said, "If you do not change, change will change you." Change constantly occurs in our jobs, locations, houses, friends, cars, clothes, and food.

These are worldly reasons for change.

"But we all, with open face beholding as in a glass the glory of the Lord, are changed into the same image from glory to glory, even as by the Spirit of the Lord" (2 Corinthians 3:18). Now this is real change!

We go to God's Word so that we may begin to comprehend Him in a new way and experience godly change inside ourselves. Being willing to change means eagerly desiring to let God's transforming light into our lives. When His light comes in, darkness leaves! Jesus is *"the light of the world."* God spoke: *"Let there be light,"* and light was!

We are to walk in the Light—in Jesus. He came that we may have life and light, and have it more abundantly. The only way we can increase in understanding is to daily read the Word of God, the Bible, so that Jesus can change us into His likeness, whole and complete in Him, the Spirit of Truth.

Hallelujah, What a Savior! He is our Savior and we can begin to become like Jesus, who is absolutely righteous and perfect. Our Savior came to completely take away our sins, never to be remembered again. So we should never let the enemy of our soul, satan, attack us by bringing up any past sins. Once you know Jesus you can tell the enemy to go see your Lord regarding accusations about your past. God won't remember any past sins! *"If we confess our sins, He is faithful and just to forgive us our sins, and to cleanse us from all unrighteousness"* (1 John 1:9).

Prayer

Savior, Author of truth and life, thank You for cleansing us and flooding us with Your glorious Light. **Hallelujah, What a Savior!**

Amen.

Have Thine Own Way, Lord

1. Have Thine own way, Lord! Have Thine own way! Thou art the Pot - ter, I am the clay. Mold me and make me Af - ter Thy will, While I am wait - ing, Yield - ed and still.
2. Have Thine own way, Lord! Have Thine own way! Search me and try me, Mas - ter, to - day! Whit - er than snow, Lord, Wash me just now, As in Thy pres - ence Hum - bly I bow.
3. Have Thine own way, Lord! Have Thine own way! Hold o'er my be - ing Ab - so - lute sway! Fill with Thy Spir - it Till all shall see Christ on - ly, al - ways, Liv - ing in me!

Have Thine Own Way, Lord

Lyrics by Adelaide A. Pollard (1862–1934)
Music by George C. Stebbins (1846–1945)

*Then I went down to the potter's house, and, behold, he wrought
a work on the wheels. And the vessel that he made of clay was
marred in the hand of the potter: so he made it again another vessel,
as seemed good to the potter to make it.*
(Jeremiah 18:3–4)

"Have Thine Own Way, Lord" was first published in 1907. In 1902 Adelaide was raising money hoping to go to Africa as a missionary. Close to the time to leave she found herself low on funds. Her deep disappointment might have caused her to lose her temper and skip a certain prayer service that was being held, but instead of allowing those feelings to guide her, she chose the positive and attended the prayer meeting! As she sat there, she overheard an elderly lady praying, saying, "It really doesn't matter what You do with us, Lord. Just have Your own way with our lives." Adelaide was so inspired by this lady that she meditated on Jeremiah 18:3, and when she arrived home she wrote the four stanzas to "**Have Thine Own Way, Lord.**"

In today's world, someone possessed of a short temper could find herself in spiritual coldness and lose the plan God has for victory in their life. What a loss they would suffer! But someone with a controlled temper, like a shiny day, leads himself and others to shed brightness over everything. Temper can cause people to speak their minds when they should be minding their speech! Ephesians 4:26 says, "*Be ye angry, and sin not: let not the sun go down upon your wrath* [anger]."

Prayer

*Please **Have Thine Own Way, Lord,** in my life. I give my temper to You to transform into kindness, love, and peacefulness. Settle and calm my thoughts. I know that if I obey Your commandments my spirit will be filled with Your holy judgments. I thank You, because I know You hear that my heart's desire is for You, Lord. Thank You.*

Amen.

The Haven of Rest

1. My soul in sad ex-ile was out on life's sea, So bur-dened with
2. I yield-ed my-self to His ten-der em-brace, In faith tak-ing
3. The song of my soul, since the Lord made me whole, Has been the old
4. How pre-cious the tho't that we all may re-cline, Like John, the be-

sin and dis-tressed, I heard a sweet voice, say-ing, "Make Me your choice;"
hold of the Word, My fet-ters fell off, and I an-chored my soul:
sto-ry so blest, Of Je-sus, who'll save who-so-ev-er will have
lov-ed and blest, On Je-sus' strong arm, where no tem-pest can harm,

Chorus

And I en-tered the Ha-ven of Rest.
The Ha-ven of Rest is my Lord.
A home in the Ha-ven of Rest.
Se-cure in the Ha-ven of Rest.

I've an-chored my soul in the

Ha-ven of Rest, I'll sail the wide seas no more; The tem-pest may

sweep o'er the wild, storm-y, deep, In Je-sus I'm safe ev-er-more.

The Haven of Rest

LYRICS BY HENRY LAKE GILMORE (1836–1920)
MUSIC BY GEORGE D. MOORE (DATES UNKNOWN)

I am the door: by Me if any man enter in, he shall be saved.
(John 10:9a)

By faith Noah, being warned of God of things not seen as yet, moved with fear [that is, respect and honor to God], *prepared an ark to the saving of his house; by the which he condemned the world, and became heir of the righteousness which is by faith.*
(Hebrews 11:7)

Some have said, "Trust in God, and all your troubles are over." This is not a true statement. Yet there is an inner peace and confidence that can be ours through our troubles when we look to our Father God, even though this is often the last thing we choose to do.

Scottish author George MacDonald once wisely wrote, "How often do we look upon God as our last and feeblest resource! We go to Him because we have nowhere else to go. And then we learn that the storms of life have driven us, not upon the rocks, but into the desired haven."[9] And that is where God could have brought us—into His will—had we only gone to Him and put our faith and trust in Him first. God is for us!

A fifth stanza of this hymn reads:

*O Come to the Savior, He patiently waits
to save by His power divine;
Come, anchor your soul in the "Haven of Rest,"
And say, "My Beloved is mine."*

Henry Lake Gilmore was born in Londonderry, Ireland, in 1836. He came to America as a youth. He served in the Civil War, was captured and had to spend time in prison in Virginia. After the war he co-founded a Methodist Church in New Jersey and brought his musical gifts to camp meetings and revivals. He published many hymn collections in his lifetime.

Prayer

Father God, as we go through the storms of life, we should always come to You first for the answers. There, Lord God, we find the calm of our Haven of Rest.

Amen.

He Keeps Me Singing
(There's Within My Heart a Melody)

1. There's with-in my heart a mel-o-dy Je-sus whis-pers
2. Feast-ing on the rich-es of His grace, Rest-ing 'neath His
3. Soon He's com-ing back to wel-come me Far be-yond the

sweet and low, Fear not, I am with thee, peace, be still,
shel-t'ring wing, Al-ways look-ing on His smil-ing face,
star-ry sky; I shall wing my flight to worlds un-known,

Chorus

In all of life's ebb and flow.
That is why I shout and sing. Je-sus, Je-sus,
I shall live with Him on high.

Je-sus, Sweet-est name I know, Fills my ev-'ry

long-ing, Keeps me sing-ing as I go.

He Keeps Me Singing
(There's Within My Heart a Melody)

Lyrics and music by Luther B. Bridgers (1884–1948)

But none saith, Where is God my maker,
who giveth songs in the night.
(Job 35:10)

I call to remembrance my song in the night: I commune with mine
own heart: and my spirit made diligent search.
(Psalm 77:6)

Luther Bridgers started to preach at age seventeen, then at eighteen years of age, he attended Asbury College in Kentucky. When he completed college he became a pastor and church planter. Soon God gave him a precious wife and three wonderful sons. Luther traveled to preach many times and on one occasion took his wife and sons to his mother- and father-in-law's home.

That evening a neighbor couldn't sleep and looked out the window, where he saw that Luther's in-laws' house was burning. The neighbor ran to sound an alarm, but meanwhile, the house was swallowed up in flames. Luther's in-laws escaped, but his wife and sons were lost in the fire. When Luther heard, there was such sadness and grief that filled his heart, it then turned to depression. But Luther knew Jesus, so depression soon had to go!

Luther recalled the Bible's promise of "*songs in the night.*" He began trusting in the power greater than himself, knowing this power would carry him through anything. He wrote "**He Keeps Me Singing**" in 1910, the year prior to his terrible loss, but only after that event did he understand that the song had been placed in his heart precisely for this time. He found peace in the midst of the storm, and he persevered in spite of tragedy. For, the enemy cannot destroy a life that is protected by faith in God.

Prayer

Thank You, my dear Father, for keeping us singing no matter what the situation, so that we overcome by our faith.

Amen.

He Leadeth Me

1. He lead - eth me: O bless-ed tho't! O words with heav-'nly com-fort fraught!
2. Some-times 'mid scenes of deep-est gloom, Some-times where E - den's bow-ers bloom,
3. Lord, I would clasp Thy hand in mine, Nor ev - er mur-mur nor re - pine,
4. And when my task on earth is done, When by Thy grace the vic-t'ry's won,

What- e'er I do, wher-e'er I be, Still 'tis God's hand that lead-eth me.
By wa - ters still, o'er trou-bled sea Still 'tis His hand that lead-eth me.
Con- tent, what-ev - er lot I see, Since 'tis my God that lead-eth me.
E'en death's cold wave I will not flee, Since God thru Jor - dan lead-eth me.

Chorus

He lead - eth me, He lead - eth me, By His own hand He lead-eth me;

His faith - ful fol-low'r I would be, For by His hand He lead-eth me.

He Leadeth Me

LYRICS BY JOSEPH HENRY GILMORE (1834–1918)
MUSIC BY WILLIAM B. BRADBURY (1816–1868)

He leadeth me in the paths of righteousness for His name's sake.
(Psalm 23:3b)

One midweek service night on March 26, 1862, Joseph Henry Gilmore was to give his congregation a message on the 23rd Psalm. As he spoke, he got no further than the words, *"He leadeth me."* He explains, "Those words took hold of me as they had never done before, and I saw in them a significance and beauty of which I had never dreamed."[10]

The story is told of a master professor of music teaching his student on the cello. The professor placed his hand on the cello and played one long and beautiful note. His student finally asked, "Sir, why are you holding your hand in the same place on the neck of the cello, while others move their hand up and down?" The professor answered, "Well, because, my dear student, I have found the place they have all been looking for!"

Sometimes it is difficult to find our place in life. In John 10:10 Jesus says, *"I am come that they might have life, and that they might have it more abundantly."* God values all of His children as dear ones. When we ask for forgiveness, He forgives and puts those sins into the sea of forgetfulness, never to be remembered again. If our enemy, satan, tries to bring that sin back to condemn you, tell him to go talk to God, your Father. God has forgiven you, and that sin was covered with the precious blood of Jesus!

Prayer

Jesus, I thank You for paying the price on the cross to remove sin from me. You are my dear Lord and Savior, who died so that I, when I die, may live eternally with You in heaven. Blessed be the glorious Name of Jesus. "He Leadeth Me"!

Amen.

Heavenly Sunlight

Heavenly Sunlight

LYRICS BY HENRY JEFFREYS ZELLEY (1859–1942)
MUSIC BY GEORGE HARRISON COOK (UNKNOWN–1948)

*Arise, shine; for thy light is come,
and the glory of the LORD is risen upon thee.*
(Isaiah 60:1)

Henry Jeffreys Zelley was a Methodist minister. He wrote "**Heaven-ly Sunlight**" in 1899, and it was first published in 1903. Reverend Zelley was born in 1859 and served in ministry for over fifty years. He wrote fifteen hundred songs and poems.

According to the Bible, Jesus is the light of the world. We are so privileged to walk through life led by Jesus' **Heavenly Sunlight**.

What does the Bible say about light? "*In the beginning,*" we read, "*God said, Let there be light: and there was light*" (Genesis 1:1, 3). From this, we understand that God created light.

Psalm 74:16 tells us, "*The day is Thine, the night also is Thine: Thou hast prepared the light and the sun.*" From this, we understand that God has authority over light.

We read in Psalm 84:11, "*For the LORD God is a sun and shield: the LORD will give grace and glory: no good thing will He withhold from them that walk uprightly.*" From this, we understand that God is like a sun to us in His provision of light and every good thing that we need.

When Jesus was transfigured on the mount, "*His face did shine as the sun*" (Matthew 17:2). He Himself is the "**Heavenly Sunlight**" that "floods our soul with glory divine," as the hymn says. We can look forward to a time in glory when the world will no longer need the sun, "*for the glory of God* [will] *lighten it, and the Lamb is the light thereof*" (Revelation 21:23).

Prayer

Father God, thank You for sending Christ Jesus to be the Light of the World, leading Your children in faith through this life, to eternal life. Thank You that Jesus is the Son of God and the true Light of this World. Lead us on, Lord, in the light!

Amen.

A sparrow sitting on a branch near a farmhouse, J. W. Whimper
(Wellcome Collection, PD)

His Eye Is on the Sparrow

LYRICS BY CIVILLA DURFEE MARTIN (1866–1948)
MUSIC BY CHARLES GABRIEL (1856–1932)

> *How amiable are Thy tabernacles, O LORD of hosts! My soul longeth,*
> *yea, even fainteth for the courts of the LORD: my heart and my flesh*
> *crieth out for the living God. Yea, the sparrow hath found an house,*
> *and the swallow a nest for herself, where she may lay her young,*
> *even Thine altars, O LORD of hosts, my King, and my God.*
> (Psalm 84:1–3)

Civilla Durfee Martin was a Canadian, born in August of 1866 in Nova Scotia. She was a music teacher. She met evangelist Dr. Walter Martin, and soon they were married. After their marriage, Civilla gave up teaching to travel and assist her husband in his ministry. Civilla tells the story of this hymn:

> Early in the spring of 1905, my husband and I were sojourning in Elmira, New York. We contracted a deep friendship for a couple by the name of Mr. and Mrs. Doolittle—true saints of God. Mrs. Doolittle had been bedridden for nigh twenty years. Her husband was an incurable cripple who had to propel himself to and from his business in a wheel chair. Despite their afflictions, they lived happy Christian lives, bringing inspiration and comfort to all who knew them. One day while we were visiting with the Doolittles, my husband commented on their bright hopefulness and asked them for the secret of it. Mrs. Doolittle's reply was simple: "His eye is on the sparrow, and I know He watches me." The beauty of this simple expression of boundless faith gripped the hearts and fired the imagination of Dr. Martin and me. The hymn "**His Eye Is on the Sparrow**" was the outcome of that experience.[11]

Prayer

Dear Lord, I know that You care about the little sparrows. Likewise, Jesus, I know that You care about me. My choices require Your wisdom. My thoughts and words require me to be obedient to You, and I pray for a clean heart so that my voice will sing, like the birds of the air, with freedom and joy.

Amen.

His Eye Is on the Sparrow

1. Why should I feel dis-courag-ed, Why should the shad-ows come,
2. "Let not your heart be troubl-ed," His ten-der word I hear,
3. When-ev-er I am tempt-ed, When-ev-er clouds a-rise,

Why should my heart be lone-ly, And long for heav'n and home,
And rest-ing on His good-ness, I lose my doubts and fears,
When songs give place to sigh-ing, when hope with-in me dies,

When Je-sus is my por-tion? My con-stant friend is He:
Tho' by the path He lead-eth, But one step I may see:
I draw the clos-er to Him; From care He sets me free;

His eye is on the spar-row, and I know He watch-es me;
His eye is on the spar-row, and I know He watch-es me;
His eye is on the spar-row, and I know He cares for me;

His eye is on the spar-row, and I know He watch-es me.
His eye is on the spar-row, and I know He watch-es me.
His eye is on the spar-row, and I know He cares for me.

His Eye Is on the Sparrow, *continued*

Chorus

I sing be-cause I'm hap-py, I sing be-cause I'm free,

I'm hap-py, I'm free,

For His eye is on the spar-row, And I know He watch-es me.

Holy, Holy, Holy

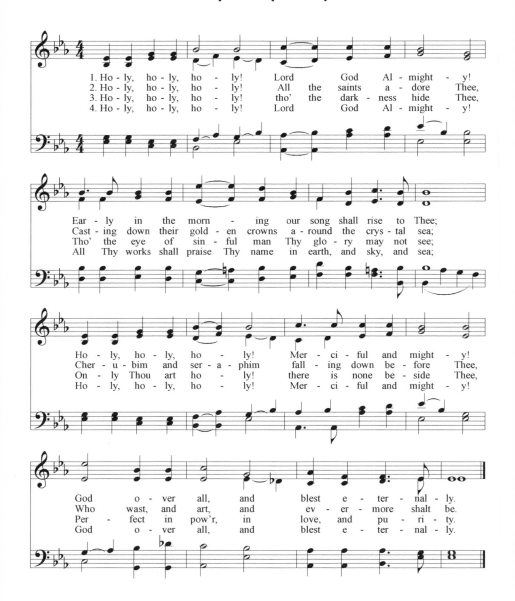

1. Ho - ly, ho - ly, ho - ly! Lord God Al - might - y!
2. Ho - ly, ho - ly, ho - ly! All the saints a - dore Thee,
3. Ho - ly, ho - ly, ho - ly! tho' the dark - ness hide Thee,
4. Ho - ly, ho - ly, ho - ly! Lord God Al - might - y!

Ear - ly in the morn - ing our song shall rise to Thee;
Cast - ing down their gold - en crowns a - round the crys - tal sea;
Tho' the eye of sin - ful man Thy glo - ry may not see;
All Thy works shall praise Thy name in earth, and sky, and sea;

Ho - ly, ho - ly, ho - ly! Mer - ci - ful and might - y!
Cher - u - bim and ser - a - phim fall - ing down be - fore Thee,
On - ly Thou art ho - ly! there is none be - side Thee,
Ho - ly, ho - ly, ho - ly! Mer - ci - ful and might - y!

God o - ver all, and blest e - ter - nal - ly.
Who wast, and art, and ev - er - more shalt be.
Per - fect in pow'r, in love, and pu - ri - ty.
God o - ver all, and blest e - ter - nal - ly.

Holy, Holy, Holy

LYRICS BY REGINALD HEBER (1783–1826)
MUSIC BY JOHN B. DYKES (1823–1876)

*I saw also the Lord sitting upon a throne, high and lifted up,
and His train filled the temple. Above it stood the seraphims…
and one cried unto another, and said, Holy, holy, holy,
is the LORD of hosts: the whole earth is full of His glory.*
(Isaiah 6:1–3)

*And the four beasts [angels] had each of them six wings about him;
…they rest not day and night, saying, Holy, holy, holy,
Lord God Almighty, which was, and is, and is to come.*
(Revelation 4:8)

We have this delightful account from hymn writer Reginald Heber's childhood:

When travelling with his parents in a very stormy day across the mountainous country between Ripon and Craven, his mother was much alarmed and proposed to leave the carriage and walk. Reginald, sitting on her knee, said—"Don't be afraid, Mama, God will take care of us." These words spoken, as she herself expressed it, by the infant monitor, carried with them conviction to her heart.… He could read the Bible with fluency at five years old, and even then was remarkable for the avidity with which he studied it, and for his accurate knowledge of its contents.[12]

The poet Alfred, Lord Tennyson is said to have considered this hymn the greatest hymn ever written in any language. It speaks of holiness. Holiness is having a commitment to a relationship with our Savior, Jesus. This is a commitment to obedience to His commandments in His Word, the Bible.

Prayer

Thank You, Lord God. When we are weary, sick, tired, and confused, we know we can come to You and call on Your holy Name for an answer to all our situations. We give You praise, for You are Holy.

Amen.

How Firm a Foundation

1. How firm a foun-da-tion, ye saints of the Lord, Is laid for your
2. "Fear not, I am with thee, O be not dis-mayed; For I am thy
3. "The soul that on Je-sus has leaned for re-pose, I will not, I

faith in His ex-cel-lent word! What more can He say than to
God, and will still give thee aid; I'll strength-en thee, help thee, and
will not de-sert to His foes; That soul, tho' all hell should en-

you He has said, You who un-to Je-sus for ref-uge have fled?
cause thee to stand, Up-held by My gra-cious, om-nip-o-tent hand."
deav-or to shake, I'll nev-er, no nev-er, no nev-er for-sake."

How Firm a Foundation

K—. (Unsure of Author)

*Nevertheless the foundation of God standeth sure, having this seal,
the Lord knoweth them that are His. And, let every one
that nameth the name of Christ depart from iniquity.*
(2 Timothy 2:19)

John Rippon loved hymns. His own hymnal, entitled *A Selection of Hymns from the Best Authors*, became a best seller among Baptist churches in America and England.

It was in Rippon's hymnal that "**How Firm a Foundation**" appeared in 1787. No one knows for certain who authored it, for in the hymnal where the author's name is normally written we find only the initial K—. It is believed that the author might have been minister of music Robert Keene.

United States Presidents Theodore Roosevelt and Woodrow Wilson, as well as General Robert E. Lee, all requested "**How Firm a Foundation**" to be sung at their funerals. It was also sung by American troops in the Spanish-American War in 1898, on Christmas eve.

This story is told in Wells's 1914 volume, *A Treasure of Hymns*:

Andrew Jackson, after retiring from the Presidency, became a devout member of the Presbyterian church. One day in his old age a company of visitors was with him, when General Jackson said, "There is a beautiful hymn on the subject of the exceeding great and precious promises of God to His people. It was a favorite hymn with my dear wife till the day of her death. It begins thus: 'How firm a foundation, ye saints of the Lord.' I wish you would sing it now." So the company did what was asked by the old hero.[13]

Prayer

*Thank You, dear God, for **How Firm a Foundation** is Jesus our Lord, upon whom we mortal humans may stand! For it is You, Lord, in whom we place our trust!*

Amen.

I Am Thine, O Lord (Draw Me Nearer)

1. I am Thine, O Lord; I have heard Thy voice, And it told Thy
2. Con - se - crate me now to Thy ser - vice, Lord, By the pow'r of
3. O the pure de - light of a sin - gle hour That be - fore Thy
4. There are depths of love that I can - not know Till I cross the

love to me, But I long to rise in the arms of faith,
grace di - vine; Let my soul look up with a stead - fast hope,
throne I spend, When I kneel in prayer, and with Thee, my God,
nar - row sea; There are heights of joy that I may not reach

Chorus

And be clos - er drawn to Thee. Draw me near - er,
And my will be lost in Thine. near - er, near - er,
I com - mune as friend with friend.
Till I rest in peace with Thee.

near - er, bless - ed Lord, To the cross where Thou hast died; Draw me near - er,

near - er, near - er, bless - ed Lord, To Thy pre - cious bleed - ing side.

I Am Thine, O Lord (Draw Me Nearer)

Lyrics by Fanny J. Crosby (1820–1915)
Music by William Howard Doane (1832–1915)

*And when he putteth forth his own sheep, he goeth before them,
and the sheep follow him: for they know his voice.
And a stranger will they not follow, but will flee from him:
for they know not the voice of strangers.*
(John 10:4–5)

William H. Doane frequently collaborated with Fanny Crosby as composer for her lyrics. We read that Crosby was considered almost as one of the Doane family. Doane's daughters referred to her as "Aunt Fanny," and she called them "little snowbirds."

During one visit by Fanny to the Doane family home in Cincinnati, they sat on Doane's porch as the sun set. Fanny was inspired with the sense of God's nearness, and was overcome by what she described as "a deep, though intangible feeling, whose expression demanded the language of poetry."[14]

Fanny once said of her blindness, "I could not have written thousands of hymns—many of which, if you will pardon me for repeating it, are sung all over the world—if I had been hindered by the distractions of seeing all the interesting and beautiful objects that would have been presented to my notice."[15]

The text for **"I Am Thine, O Lord"** was taken from Hebrews 10:22: *"Let us draw near with a true heart in full assurance of faith, having our hearts sprinkled from an evil conscience, and our bodies washed with pure water."*

Prayer

*"**I Am Thine, O Lord**, I have heard Thy voice, and it told Thy love to me; But I long to rise in the arms of faith and be closer drawn to Thee." This is the cry of my heart, for I am Yours and I want to be drawn closer to You, my sweet Lord!*

I Love to Tell the Story

1. I love to tell the story Of unseen things above, Of Jesus and His glory, Of Jesus and His love; I love to tell the story Because I know 'tis true; It satisfies my longings As nothing else can do.

2. I love to tell the story; 'Tis pleasant to repeat What seems, each time I tell it, More wonderfully sweet; I love to tell the story, For some have never heard The message of salvation From God's own holy word.

3. I love to tell the story, For those who know it best Seem hungering and thirsting To hear it like the rest; And when, in scenes of glory, I sing the new, new song, 'Twill be the old, old story That I have loved so long.

Chorus

I love to tell the story! 'Twill be my theme in glory To tell the old, old story Of Jesus and His love.

I Love to Tell the Story

Lyrics by Arabella Katherine Hankey (1834–1911)
Music by William G. Fischer (1835–1912)

*And thou shalt love the Lord thy God with all thine heart,
and with all thy soul, and with all thy might.*
(Deuteronomy 6:5)

Arabella Katherine Hankey suffered from a serious illness when she was thirty-two years of age. During her long recovery, she composed a fifty-stanza poem that expressed all that she was going through. Two separate hymns were composed using different stanzas from Hankey's heartfelt poem, one of them being "Tell Me the Old, Old Story," put to music by William Howard Doane, and the other being this hymn.

A story is told by Ira Sankey of an unnamed young man of exemplary godly behavior seeking to teach temperance amongst his fellows:

> While here he went to church, and the curate, who had a conversation with him, was much pleased with his manly behaviour and resolute desire to do right. He wore a medal and had good conduct marks on his clothes. This man was the little boy…picked up in Battersea Park many years before, and who had learned of the Gospel of salvation entirely from listening to the maidservants singing sacred songs while scrubbing doorsteps and cleaning windows. The hymn that, as a child, he seemed to make entirely his own was, "**I Love to Tell the Story**."… As he had never been to church or chapel, the hymns were the only channel through which Divine truth had been conveyed to him, and by which the first seed was sown in his heart that made him a man of character and usefulness.[16]

It has been said that prosperity is neither being rich nor being poor, but it is that the spirit of the person is prosperous. Material wealth comes and goes, but God's Word never fails; it lasts eternally!

Prayer

Lord, we are taught that eternity is long, and these days of this life are very few. Help and teach us, Holy Spirit, to know how to be faithful to You in what we think and in our actions. Let our lives glorify and honor You, Lord, in everything we say and do.

73

I Need Thee Every Hour

1. I need Thee ev - 'ry hour, Most gra - cious Lord;
2. I need Thee ev - 'ry hour, Stay Thou near - by;
3. I need Thee ev - 'ry hour, Most Ho - ly One;

No ten - der voice like Thine Can peace af - ford.
Temp - ta - tions lose their pow'r When Thou art nigh.
O make me Thine in - deed, Thou bless - ed Son!

Chorus

I need Thee, O I need Thee; Ev - 'ry hour I need Thee! O
bless me now, my Sav - ior; I come to Thee!

74

I Need Thee Every Hour

Lyrics by Annie S. Hawks (1835–1918)
Music by Robert Lowry (1826–1899)

*Not that we are sufficient of ourselves to think any thing
as of ourselves; but our sufficiency is of God.*
(2 Corinthians 3:5)

Annie Hawks tells of how this hymn came to be:

One day as a young wife and mother of 37 years of age, I was busy with my regular household tasks during a bright June morning, in 1872. Suddenly, I became filled with the sense of nearness to the Master, and I began to wonder how anyone could ever live without Him, either in joy or pain. Then, the words were ushered into my mind and these thoughts took full possession of me—"I need Thee every hour…"

Later in her life, Annie suffered the loss of her husband, and by God's grace was ministered to by her own song:

I did not understand at first why this hymn had touched the great throbbing heart of humanity. It was not until long years after, when the shadow fell over my way, the shadow of a great loss, that I understood something of the comforting power in the words, which I had been permitted to give out to others in my hour of sweet serenity and peace.[17]

*Dearest Father, I thank You for Mrs. Annie Hawks, for the special moment during her busy life at age thirty-seven with husband and children, when she felt Your presence in her heart in such a tender way that she knew she could not live without Jesus, either in joy or in pain. As for me, **I Need Thee Every Hour**, most precious Lord. I thank You for my salvation, in Jesus' Name.*

Amen.

I Sing the Mighty Power of God

1. I sing the might-y pow'r of God, That made the moun-tains rise;
2. I sing the good-ness of the Lord, That filled the earth with food;
3. There's not a plant or flow'r be-low, But makes Thy glo-ries known;

That spread the flow-ing seas a-broad, And built the loft-y skies.
He formed the crea-tures with His word, And then pro-nounced them good.
And clouds a-rise, and tem-pests blow, By or-der from Thy throne;

I sing the wis-dom that or-dained The sun to rule the day;
Lord, how Thy won-ders are dis-played, Wher-e'er I turn my eye:
While all that bor-rows life from Thee Is ev-er in Thy care,

The moon shines full at His com-mand, And all the stars o-bey.
If I sur-vey the ground I tread, Or gaze up-on the sky!
And ev-'ry-where that we can be, Thou, God art pres-ent there.

I Sing the Mighty Power of God

LYRICS BY ISAAC WATTS (1674–1748)
MUSIC FROM GESANGBUCH DER HERZOGL

And, behold, I send the promise of My Father upon you:
but tarry ye in the city of Jerusalem, until ye be endued
with power from on high.
(Luke 24:49)

Isaac Watts is considered the father of English-language hymn writing. Many hymns that we hold dear even today came from his pen, including "When I Survey the Wondrous Cross" and the Christmas favorite "Joy to the World." He preached and also wrote many books, but his hymn writing is his greatest legacy.

As a young man, Watts served as a pastor in London. He was sickly, and his church took very good care of their beloved pastor. We read that "one day, when Watts was sick, Sir Thomas Abney invited him to his splendid home for a week. He became so dear to the household that they kept him there for the rest of his life,—thirty-six years!"

"**I Sing the Mighty Power of God**" was written for Watts's hymnal *Hymns and Spiritual Songs*. He also wrote songs for children, although he did not have any of his own. It was said of him: "Well did he know the child's heart."[18]

Isaac Watts died in 1748 and is buried near the grave of John Bunyan, author of the Christian allegorical book *The Pilgrim's Progress.*

In Matthew 19:13–14 this story is told about Jesus: "*Then were there brought unto Him little children, that He should put His hands on them, and pray: and the disciples rebuked them. But Jesus said, Suffer little children, and forbid them not, to come unto me: for of such is the kingdom of heaven.*"

Prayer

Lord, bless our children and grandchildren and great grandchildren whom we love and whom You, Lord, have given to us as precious gifts. May we show wisdom and extreme love for them as they learn. May we never show anger when they miss the mark but show care for them, because, Lord, we miss it too, and You lift us into Your arms with extreme love repeatedly until we get it! Thank You, Lord.

Amen.

I Surrender All (All to Jesus I Surrender)

1. All to Je - sus, I sur - ren - der, All to Him I free - ly give;
2. All to Je - sus, I sur - ren - der, Humb - ly at His feet I bow;
3. All to Je - sus, I sur - ren - der, Make me, Sav - ior, whol - ly Thine;
4. All to Je - sus, I sur - ren - der, Lord, I give my - self to Thee;

I will ev - er love and trust Him, In His pres - ence dai - ly live.
World - ly pleas - ures all for - sak - en, Take me, Je - sus, take me now.
Let me know the joy of liv - ing, Tru - ly know that Thou art mine.
Fill me with Thy love and pow - er, Let Thy bless - ings fall on me.

Chorus

I sur - ren - der all, I sur - ren - der all;
I sur - ren - der all, I sur - ren - der all;

All to Thee, my bles - sed Sav - ior, I sur - ren - der all.

I Surrender All (All to Jesus I Surrender)

LYRICS BY JUDSON W. VAN DEVENTER (1855–1939)
MUSIC BY WINFIELD S. WEEDEN (1847–1908)

But now, O LORD, Thou art our Father; we are the clay,
and Thou our potter; and we all are the work of Thy hand.
(Isaiah 64:8)

Someone once said that only in the Christian does surrender bring victory. Judson Wheeler Van DeVenter was born on a farm in late 1855 near Dundee, Michigan. Judson was interested in art and music. He was converted at age seventeen.

Van DeVenter tells us about how this hymn came to be:

> For some time, I had struggled between developing my talents in the field of art and going into full-time evangelistic work. At last the pivotal hour of my life came, and I surrendered all. A new day was ushered into my life. I became an evangelist and discovered down deep in my soul a talent hitherto unknown to me. God had hidden a song in my heart, and touching a tender chord, He caused me to sing.

Dr. Billy Graham wrote of Van DeVenter, "One of the evangelists who influenced my early preaching was also a hymnist who wrote, 'I Surrender All'—the Rev. J. W. Van DeVenter.... We students loved this kind, deeply spiritual gentleman and often gathered in his winter home at Tampa, Florida, for an evening of fellowship and singing."[19]

When we **Surrender All** to Jesus, we can be assured that our lives are in the best of hands. By allowing Him to be our "blessed Savior," we can find true "joy of living." In surrendering all, we gain all!

Prayer

Thank You, God, that You have given many talents to so many people and to me too. Whatever talents I have came as Your gift. Please help me to hear Your voice to increase my talent and ability to serve You!

Amen.

In the Garden (I Come to the Garden Alone)

1. I come to the gar - den a - lone, While the dew is still on the ros - es; And the voice I hear, Fall - ing on my ear, The Son of God dis - clos - es.

2. He speaks, and the sound of His voice, Is so sweet the birds hush their sing - ing; And the mel - o - dy That He gave to me, With - in my heart is ring - ing.

3. I'd stay in the gar - den with Him, Tho the night a - round me be fall - ing, But He bids me go; Thru the voice of woe His voice to me is call - ing.

Chorus

And He walks with me, and He talks with me, And He tells me I am His own; And the joy we share as we tar - ry there, None oth - er has ev - er known.

In the Garden (I Come to the Garden Alone)

LYRICS AND MUSIC BY CHARLES AUSTIN MILES (1868–1946)

For ye have the poor with you always,… but Me ye have not always.
(Mark 14:7)

Charles Austin Miles was born in Lakehurst, New Jersey, in 1868. Miles attended the Philadelphia College of Pharmacy and the University of Pennsylvania. He abandoned his profession as a pharmacist in 1892 and wrote his first gospel song, "List! 'Tis Jesus' Voice," which was published by Hall-Mack Publishing Company, where he went on to work as editor and manager for thirty-seven years. Miles says, "It is as a writer of gospel songs I am proud to be known, for in that way I may be of the most use to my Master, whom I serve willingly although not as efficiently as is my desire."[20]

The reference to the garden becomes so much easier to understand when we recognize that Charles Austin Miles was writing about the first Resurrection (Easter) morning, referring to the garden in which Jesus was buried. Mary Magdalene goes there alone, very early—that is, "while the dew was still on the roses." When Jesus first speaks to her, she thinks it is the gardener, but when He calls her by name, she recognizes His voice.

When our lives take an unexpected and unwelcome turn to hardships such as a heart-breaking diagnosis, a financial disaster, a wreck, or a death, we must exercise our faith. As Christians, we are not alone. God always goes ahead of us to prepare the way so that we can overcome. He is present in our difficulties with grace, mercy, and supernatural wisdom. He will ensure that our needs are met and bring us victory in Jesus.

Prayer

*Dear Lord, we are so joyful to be able to tarry **In the Garden** with You! Thank You for growing our faith and trust in You to bring about anointed and victorious answers that supply our needs and the needs of others.*

Amen.

It Is Well with My Soul

1. When peace like a riv - er at - tend - eth my way, When sor - rows like
2. My sin— Oh, the bliss of this glo - ri - ous tho't— My sin, not in
(faster) 3. And, Lord, haste the day when the faith shall be sight, The clouds be rolled

sea - bil - lows roll; What ev - er my lot, Thou hast taught me to say,
part but the whole, Is nailed to the cross and I bear it no more;
back as a scroll, The trump shall re - sound and the Lord shall de - scend,

(cues: vs. 3 only)

Chorus

"It is well, it is well with my soul." It is well It is well
Praise the Lord, praise the Lord, O my soul! It is well
"E - ven so" it is well with my soul.

with my soul, It is well, it is well with my soul.
with my soul,

It Is Well with My Soul

LYRICS BY HORATIO G. SPAFFORD (1828–1888)
MUSIC BY PHILLIP P. BLISS (1838–1876)

Many are the afflictions of the righteous:
but the LORD delivereth him out of them all.
(Psalm 34:19)

oratio G. Spafford was a successful senior partner in a Chicago law firm. Throughout his life he faced many tragedies that a weaker man would not have survived.

The Great Fire of Chicago of 1871 wiped out his real estate holdings, destroying him financially. He lost a child to scarlet fever. In 1873 he and his family planned a trip to Europe, but at the last minute he had to remain behind for business. He sent his wife, Anna, and four daughters on ahead. While crossing the Atlantic, their ship, the *Ville du Havre*, was struck by an English iron sailing vessel. Water poured into the ship. The *Ville du Havre* passengers were swept into the dark, icy waters. The ship sank quickly, resulting in the loss of 226 people, including Spafford's four daughters. When they reached England, Spafford's wife sent him a telegraph that read, "Saved alone."

Spafford immediately boarded a ship to reunite with Anna. He asked the captain to point out where his four daughters had gone down. He stood on the deck and contemplated this terrible wreck that had taken his girls. But his faith held him fast to the Lord, knowing they were not at the bottom of the ocean, but in the arms of their Heavenly Father. Spafford wrote "**It Is Well with My Soul**" on that very difficult journey.

It is tempting to focus on tragedy in the lives of those who have suffered a great deal, but it may be more appropriate to think of survivors like Horatio Spafford as overcomers who triumph over tragedy.[21]

Prayer

Dear Father, let us be strong in the Lord and the power of Your might when tragedies overtake us and leave us weak and faithless. Let us remember this story, that we might be sustained by our faith and know that God is God, and has the answer for every situation in our lives.

Amen.

Ivory Palaces

1. My Lord has gar-ments so won-drous fine, And myrrh their tex-ture fills;
2. His life had al-so its sor-rows sore, For al-oes had a part;
3. In gar-ments glo-ri-ous He will come, To o-pen wide the door;

Its fra-grance reached to this heart of mine With joy my be-ing thrills.
And when I think of the cross He bore, My eyes with tear-drops start.
And I shall en-ter my heav'n-ly home To dwell for-ev-er-more.

Chorus

Out of the i-vo-ry pal-a-ces, In-to a world of woe,

Rit...

On-ly His great e-ter-nal love Made my Sav-ior go.

Ivory Palaces

LYRICS AND MUSIC BY HENRY BARRACLOUGH (1891–1983)

Thou art fairer than the children of men: grace is poured into Thy lips: therefore God hath blessed Thee for ever.
(Psalm 45:2)

All Thy garments smell of myrrh, and aloes, and cassia, out of the ivory palaces, whereby they have made Thee glad.
(Psalm 45:8)

Evangelist Dr. J. Wilbur Chapman was preaching at the Montreat, North Carolina, Presbyterian Conference Center in 1915. Assisting were song leader Charles Alexander, soloist Albert Brown, and young pianist Henry Barraclough. One evening Dr. Chapman spoke on Psalm 45. At the conclusion of the meeting, young Henry was driving away from the meeting, when a new song began to form in his mind. He had nothing to write on, so he scribbled the refrain on a business card. At his hostel, he added the first three stanzas and the music. That song was sung the very next morning at the conference. At Dr. Chapman's request, Henry added a fourth stanza about the second coming of Christ. [22]

In Psalm 45:7 we read that God has anointed the king *"with the oil of gladness above Thy fellows."* The myrrh and cassia that we read about in the following verse, Psalm 45:8, mentioned in this hymn, were two of the principal ingredients of that anointing oil. Israel used them to anoint kings and priests during their inaugurations. Myrrh and aloes are used to describe the beloved bride in Song of Solomon 4:14. The spices that perfumed the king's robes were also brought by the wise men as gifts to commemorate the birth of Jesus. Furthermore, we find that myrrh and aloes were also used for Jesus' burial (John 19:39).

Out of the Ivory Palaces, into a world of woe, only His great eternal love made my Savior go.

Prayer

How awesome is Your love for us, that compelled You to leave Your heavenly dwelling just for us! Let us be filled with faith and covered with Your Love, Lord, as we serve You with all of our hearts.

Amen.

Jesus Is All the World to Me

1. Je-sus is all the world to me, My life, my joy, my all;
2. Je-sus is all the world to me, My Friend in tri-als sore;
3. Je-sus is all the world to me, I want no bet-ter Friend;

He is my strength from day to day With-out Him I would fall.
I go to Him for bless-ings, and He gives them o'er and o'er.
I trust Him now, I'll trust Him when Life's fleet-ing days shall end.

When I am sad to Him I go; No oth-er one can cheer me so;
He sends the sun-shine and the rain; He sends the har-vest's gold-en grain;
Beau-ti-ful life with such a Friend, Beau-ti-ful life that has no end;

When I am sad He makes me glad: He's my Friend.
Sun-shine and rain, har-vest of grain, He's my Friend.
E - ter-nal life, e - ter - nal joy: He's my Friend.

Jesus Is All the World to Me

LYRICS AND MUSIC BY WILL LAMARTINE THOMPSON (1847–1909)

For what is a man advantaged, if he gain the whole world,
and lose himself, or be cast away?
(Luke 9:25)

W ill L. Thompson wrote these wonderful words:

Jesus Is All the World to Me, *my life, my joy, my all;*
He is my strength from day to day, without Him I would fall.
When I am sad, to Him I go, no other one can cheer me so;
when I am sad, He makes me glad, He's my friend.

Jesus is all the world to me, my Friend in trials sore;
I go to Him for blessings, and He gives them o'er and o'er.
He sends the sunshine and the rain, He sends the harvest's golden grain;
sunshine and rain, harvest of grain, He's my friend.

Thompson began writing as a very young man. He graduated college with a business degree from Mount Union College in Alliance, Ohio. Later, he graduated from the Boston and the New England Conservatories of Music, and even studied music in Leipzig, Germany.

While attending an evangelistic service by D. L. Moody, Thompson made the decision to devote his life to writing and promoting Christian music. He wrote "Softly and Tenderly Jesus Is Calling" in 1880, which quickly became a popular invitation hymn. He wrote "**Jesus Is All the World to Me**" in 1904 and it became quite popular as well. Even though he became rich he always gave generously and lived a life of continual service to God.

Prayer

Jesus, when I sing the words of these wonderful songs, I know that You are my dearest friend. If I learn to follow You I can also be a great friend to others, and share how wonderful it is to have a loving friend with whom to share eternity. Thank You, Jesus.

Amen.

Jesus, Lover of My Soul

1. Je - sus, Lov - er of my soul, Let me to Thy bos - om fly,
2. Oth - er ref - uge have I none, Hangs my help - less soul on Thee;
3. Plen - teous grace with Thee is found, Grace to cov - er all my sin;

While the near - er wa - ters roll, While the tem - pest still is high;
Leave, O leave me not a - lone, Still sup - port and com - fort me;
Let the heal - ing streams a - bound, Make and keep me pure with - in;

Hide me, O my Sav - ior, hide, Till the storm of life is past;
All my trust on Thee is stayed; All my help from Thee I bring;
Thou of life the foun - tain art; Free - ly let me take of Thee;

Safe in - to the ha - ven guide, O re - ceive my soul at last.
Cov - er my de - fense - less head With the shad - ow of Thy wing.
Spring Thou up with - in my heart, Rise to all e - ter - ni - ty.

Jesus, Lover of My Soul

LYRICS AND MUSIC BY CHARLES WESLEY (1707–1788)

Love worketh no ill to his neighbor:
therefore love is the fulfilling of the law.
(Romans 13:10)

And we have known and believed the love that God hath to us.
God is love; and he that dwelleth in love dwelleth in God,
and God in him.
(1 John 4:16)

We have this wonderful story from Ira Sankey:

A Confederate soldier had aimed his rifle and was about to shoot through the heart a Unionist sentry when he was stopped short by hearing his intended victim singing the lines "Cover my defenceless head, with the shadow of thy wing." Nearly 30 years later the Confederate veteran recognized the voice of the man whose life he had spared singing the same hymn on an excursion steamer on the Potomac River. He went up and told him how and why his life had been spared.[23]

"Now thanks be unto God, which always causeth us to triumph in Christ, and maketh manifest the savour of His knowledge by us in every place. For we are unto God a sweet savour of Christ, in them that are saved, and in them that perish" (2 Corinthians 2:14–15).

Wells, in his *A Treasure of Hymns* writes, "The three greatest hymn-writers of our English tongue are Isaac Watts, Charles Wesley, and Fanny Crosby. There are many who think that the hymn we are to study ["**Jesus, Lover of My Soul**"] is the greatest hymn ever written; all men agree that it is the best of Wesley's hymns."[24]

Prayer

Lord, when we are called to go and tell others about salvation through Christ, encourage us to go and share, fast and pray, and give to the Kingdom of God, then to rest in the hope that the Holy Spirit will win someone to everlasting life in Christ.

Amen.

Jesus Loves Me

1. Je - sus loves me! this I know, For the Bi - ble tells me so;
2. Je - sus loves me! He who died, Heav - en's gate to o - pen wide;
3. Je - sus, take this heart of mine, Make it pure and whol - ly Thine;

Lit - tle ones to Him be - long, They are weak but He is strong.
He will wash a - way my sin, Let His lit - tle child come in.
Thou hast bled and died for me, I will hence - forth live for Thee.

Chorus

Yes, Je - sus loves me; Yes, Je - sus loves me;

Yes, Je - sus loves me; The Bi - ble tells me so.

Jesus Loves Me

LYRICS BY ANNA BARTLETT WARNER (1824–1915)
MUSIC AND REFRAIN BY WILLIAM B. BRADBURY (1816–1868)

*Thou shalt not avenge, nor bear any grudge against the children of
thy people, but thou shalt love thy neighbor as thyself: I am the LORD.*
(Leviticus 19:18)

*This is my commandment, That ye love one another,
as I have loved you. Greater love hath no man than this,
that a man lay down his life for his friends.*
(John 15:12–13)

Anna Bartlett Warner and her sister Sarah lived in a lovely home in
New York City, where their father was a successful lawyer. When
the "Panic of 1837" wrecked the family's finances, they had to move to
their old summer farmhouse across the river from West Point Military
Academy.

Anna and Susan began to write poems and stories for publication
to contribute to the family income. One of their novels, *Say and Seal*,
features a dying boy whose Sunday School teacher holds the boy in
his arms. To comfort him he sings to the boy, "Jesus loves me, this I
know, for the Bible tells me so…" This best-selling novel was second
only to *Uncle Tom's Cabin*. When hymn writer William Bradbury read
the words of the little song, he composed a musical score for it. Ryden,
writing in 1930 in *The Story of Our Hymns*, writes, "We wonder if any
child in America during the last half century has not learned to know
and to love the little hymn—'Jesus loves me, this I know, For the Bible
tells me so.'"[25]

For forty years, Susan and Anna conducted Bible studies for the
cadets at West Point. When the sisters passed away they were buried
with full military honors, and are the only civilians buried in the military cemetery at West Point.

Prayer

*Lord, we thank You for Anna Warner, who listened to Your call to
write "Jesus Loves Me" and other blessed songs. Lord, when You call,
may we act immediately as Your Holy Spirit speaks to our hearts, leading our paths. We love You, Lord.*

Amen.

Jesus Paid It All

1. I hear the Sav - ior say, "Thy strength in - deed is small;
2. Lord, now in - deed I find Thy pow'r, and Thine a - lone,
3. And when be - fore the throne I stand in Him com - plete,

Child of weak - ness, watch and pray, Find in Me thine all in all."
Can change the lep - er's spots, And melt the heart of stone.
I'll lay my tro - phies down, All down at Je - sus' feet.

Chorus

Je - sus paid it all, All to Him I owe;

Sin had left a crim - son stain, He washed it white as snow.

Jesus Paid It All

LYRICS BY ELVINA HALL (1820–1889)
MUSIC BY GEORGE T. GRAPE (1835–1915)

Let us hold fast the profession of our faith without wavering;
(for He is faithful that promised).
(Hebrews 10:23)

One Sunday at Monument Street Methodist Church in Baltimore, Mrs. Elvina Hall sat in her regular seat in the choir loft as the Rev. George Schrick was going on and on with his rather lengthy and pious prayer. Suddenly, words began pouring into her heart. She wrote them down in the margin of her hymnal, not having any other paper available. Later, Elvira delivered her poem into her good Reverend's hands.

Prior to that day, Rev. Schrick had received a melody composed without lyrics from another congregant by the name of George Grape. Grape was a coal merchant who served as organist at the church. A melody that lacked inspired lyrics and lyrics that needed to come alive in song were brought together by God's providence. God worked through Mrs. Hall, Mr. Grape, and Rev. Schrick to synthesize with perfect balance this special hymn **"Jesus Paid It All."**

And now complete in Him, my robe, His righteousness,

Close sheltered, 'neath His side, I am divinely blest,

When from my dying bed My ransomed soul shall rise,

"Jesus died my soul to save," shall rend the vaulted skies.

Many of the lyrics of this hymn have been changed through the years to make them more singable and give more clarity to the song, but the promise remains the same: that **"Jesus Paid It All."**

Prayer

Dear Jesus, we bless You for paying the price for our salvation by shedding Your blood and dying on the cross for the forgiveness of our sin. We thank You, our glorious Lord Jesus!

Amen.

Jesus Saves!
(We Have Heard the Joyful Sound)

1. We have heard the joy - ful sound: Je - sus saves! Je - sus saves!
2. Waft it on the roll - ing tide: Je - sus saves! Je - sus saves!
3. Sing a - bove the bat - tle strife: Je - sus saves! Je - sus saves!
4. Give the winds a might - y voice: Je - sus saves! Je - sus saves!

Spread the tid - ings all a - round: Je - sus saves! Je - sus saves!
Tell to sin - ners far and wide: Je - sus saves! Je - sus saves!
By His death and end - less life, Je - sus saves! Je - sus saves!
Let the na - tions now re - joice: Je - sus saves! Je - sus saves!

Bear the news to ev - 'ry land, Climb the steeps and cross the waves;
Sing, ye is - lands of the sea; Ech - o back, ye o - cean caves;
Sing it soft - ly thro' the gloom, When the heart for mer - cy craves;
Shout sal - va - tion full and free, High - est hills and deep - est caves;

On - ward! 'tis our Lord's com - mand: Je - sus saves! Je - sus saves!
Earth shall keep her ju - bi - lee: Je - sus saves! Je - sus saves!
Sing in tri - umph o'er the tomb: Je - sus saves! Je - sus saves!
This our song of vic - to - ry: Je - sus saves! Je - sus saves!

Jesus Saves!
(We Have Heard the Joyful Sound)

LYRICS BY PRISCILLA JANE OWENS (1829–1907)
MUSIC BY JOSIAH BOOTH (1852–1929)

For the Son of man is come to save that which was lost.
(Matthew 18:11)

Priscilla J. Owens was born in 1829. She was a teacher in Baltimore for most of her life and served in Sunday school for fifty years as a member of the Union Square Methodist Episcopal Church. Most of her songs were written for children's services.

This hymn appeared in the *Scotch Church Hymnary* of 1898 under the name, **"We Have Heard the Joyful Sound,"** which is the first line of this wonderful song for missions, written for a Sunday school mission anniversary.

What does it mean that **"Jesus Saves"**? The New Testament uses words such as *save, saved, salvation,* and *Saviour* (King James spelling) nearly two hundred times. By far the majority relate to the salvation offered through faith in the work of Jesus.

Luke and John relate the following: *"For mine eyes have seen Thy salvation," "for unto you is born this day in the city of David a Saviour, which is Christ the Lord." "For God sent not His Son into the world to condemn the world; but that the world through Him might be saved." "Jesus saith unto him, I am the way, the truth, and the life: no man cometh unto the Father, but by Me"* (Luke 2:30, 11; John 3:17, 14:6).

Prayer

Dear Lord, **We Have Heard the Joyful Sound: Jesus Saves, Jesus Saves!** *Thank You, our wonderful Savior, that the true sound over which we rejoice is Your gift of salvation. For if we ask You to remove the sin from our lives and replace it with everlasting life, then we will live eternally in heaven, praising God with You. Thank You, Lord!*

Amen.

Joyful, Joyful, We Adore Thee

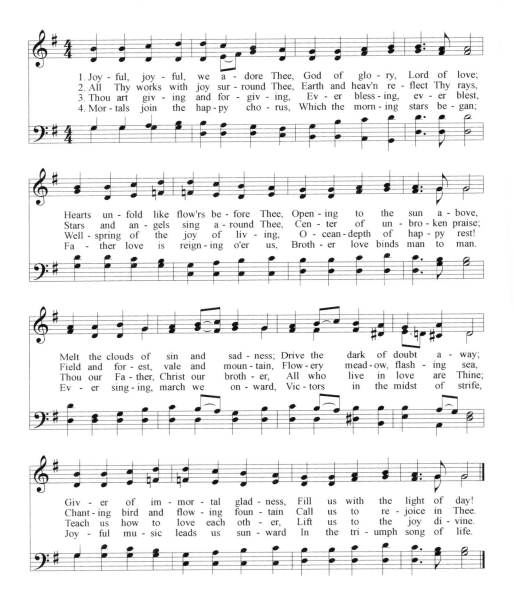

1. Joy - ful, joy - ful, we a - dore Thee, God of glo - ry, Lord of love;
2. All Thy works with joy sur - round Thee, Earth and heav'n re - flect Thy rays,
3. Thou art giv - ing and for - giv - ing, Ev - er bless - ing, ev - er blest,
4. Mor - tals join the hap - py cho - rus, Which the morn - ing stars be - gan;

Hearts un - fold like flow'rs be - fore Thee, Open - ing to the sun a - bove,
Stars and an - gels sing a - round Thee, Cen - ter of un - bro - ken praise;
Well - spring of the joy of liv - ing, O - cean - depth of hap - py rest!
Fa - ther love is reign - ing o'er us, Broth - er love binds man to man.

Melt the clouds of sin and sad - ness; Drive the dark of doubt a - way;
Field and for - est, vale and moun - tain, Flow - ery mead - ow, flash - ing sea,
Thou our Fa - ther, Christ our broth - er, All who live in love are Thine;
Ev - er sing - ing, march we on - ward, Vic - tors in the midst of strife,

Giv - er of im - mor - tal glad - ness, Fill us with the light of day!
Chant - ing bird and flow - ing foun - tain Call us to re - joice in Thee.
Teach us how to love each oth - er, Lift us to the joy di - vine.
Joy - ful mu - sic leads us sun - ward In the tri - umph song of life.

Joyful, Joyful, We Adore Thee

LYRICS BY HENRY VAN DYKE (1852–1933)
MUSIC BY LUDWIG VAN BEETHOVEN (1770–1827)

Make a joyful noise unto God, all ye lands.
(Psalm 66:1)

Are not five sparrows sold for two farthings [half of an old penny],
and not one of them is forgotten before God?
But even the very hairs of your head are all numbered.
Fear not therefore: ye are of more value than many sparrows.
Also I say unto you, Whosoever shall confess me before men,
him shall the Son of man also confess before the angels of God.
(Luke 12:6–8)

The music for this hymn is taken from the familiar "Ode to Joy" melody from the last movement of Beethoven's Ninth Symphony. The lyrics by Henry Van Dyke were inspired by the Berkshire Mountains, as Van Dyke was a guest preacher at Williams College in the Berkshires. We see mention of flowers, sun, forest, vale, mountain, meadow, and sea, all calling us "to rejoice in Thee."

Here are Van Dyke's own words about the writing of this hymn:

These verses are simple expressions of common Christian feelings and desires in this present time, hymns of today that may be sung together by people who know the thought of the age, and are not afraid that any truth of science will destroy their religion or that any revolution on earth will overthrow the kingdom of heaven. Therefore these are hymns of trust and hope.[26]

Father God, we know that "the fruit of righteousness is sown in peace of them that make peace" (James 3:18). As we go through each day, may we, when we encounter anger, envy, contentiousness, or provoking, sow seeds of peace, joy, and love. May our personality and character reflect Yours, dear God.

Just a Closer Walk with Thee

1. I am weak but Thou art strong; Je - sus, keep me from all wrong.
2. Thru this world of toil and snares, If I fal - ter, Lord, who cares?
3. When my fee - ble life is o'er, Time for me will be no more,

I'll be sat - is - fied as long As I walk, dear Lord, close to Thee.
Who with me my bur - den shares? None but Thee, dear Lord, none but Thee.
Guide me gen - tly, safe - ly o'er To Thy king - dom shore, to Thy shore.

Chorus

Just a clos - er walk with Thee, Grant it, Je - sus, is my plea.

Dai - ly walk - ing close to Thee, Let it be, dear Lord, let it be.

Just a Closer Walk with Thee

Author unknown

And whatsoever we ask, we receive of Him, because we keep His commandments, and do those things that are pleasing in His sight.
(1 John 3:22)

I believe that we must read God's Word. We need to know what 1 John 4:9 says: "*In this was manifested the love of God toward us, because that God sent His only begotten Son into the world, that we might live through Him.*"

In this song, we acknowledge our human inability to live a totally righteous life, and we also express awareness of God's grace and strength given to us daily as we walk by faith in Him. "*And He* [God] *said unto me* [Paul], *'My grace is sufficient for thee: for My strength is made perfect in weakness.'... Therefore I take pleasure in...distresses for Christ's sake: for when I am weak, then am I strong*" (2 Corinthians 12:9–10).

When we desire, Lord, **Just a Closer Walk with Thee**, *we must pray and read the Bible—Your Word.* God says in His Word, "*The Word was made flesh, and dwelt among us*" (John 1:14). Jesus *is* the Word; if we want a closer walk with Jesus, our Savior, we must study the Word!

Furthermore, you cannot become like Jesus or develop His character unless you spend time with the One you admire and are devoted to! When we are obedient, we are blessed. Sometimes our "**Closer Walk with Thee**" may even bring persecution our way. "*Blessed are they which are persecuted for righteousness' sake: for theirs is the kingdom of heaven*" (Matthew 5:10).

Faith is not believing in spite of evidence; it is obeying in spite of consequence.[27] Faith is simply obeying God. As it is said, faith hears the inaudible; faith sees the invisible; faith believes the incredible; faith receives the impossible. When we do what we can by faith, God will fill in the gaps. Faith to do the right thing can rewrite your future.

Prayer

Father, we don't know the author of this hymn, but we do know that the author knew You. For the Bible says that if we draw nigh to You, then You will draw nigh to us (James 4:8).

Amen.

Just As I Am

1. Just as I am, with-out one plea, But that Thy blood was shed for me,
2. Just as I am, and wait-ing not To rid my soul of one dark blot,
3. Just as I am, tho' tossed a-bout With man-y a con-flict, man-y a doubt,
4. Just as I am- Thou wilt re-ceive, Wilt wel-come, par-don, cleanse, re-lieve;

And that Thou bidd'st me come to Thee, O Lamb of God, I come! I come!
To Thee whose blood can cleanse each spot, O Lamb of God, I come! I come!
Fight-ings and fears with-in with-out, O Lamb of God, I come! I come!
Be-cause Thy prom-ise I be-lieve, O Lamb of God, I come! I come!

A child with its mother saying a prayer at night

Just As I Am

Lyrics by Charlotte Elliott (1789–1871)
Music by William B. Bradbury (1816–1868)

*I am the vine, ye are the branches: He that abideth in Me,
and I in him, the same bringeth forth much fruit:
for without Me ye can do nothing.*
(John 15:5)

The author of the hymn "**Just As I Am**," Charlotte Elliott, had been a woman of intelligence and activity. But Charlotte was struck with an illness and had to reevaluate herself and what she had to offer in service to God. Ira Sankey tells this story:

> Miss Charlotte Elliott was visiting some friends in the West End of London, and there met the eminent minister, César Malan. While seated at supper, the minister said he hoped that she was Christian. She took offence at this, and replied that she would rather not discuss that question. Dr. Malan said that he was sorry if he had offended her, that he always liked to speak a word for his Master, and that he hoped that the young lady would some day become a worker for Christ. When they met again at the home of a mutual friend, three weeks later, Miss Elliott told the minister that ever since he had spoken to her she had been trying to find her Saviour, and that she now wished him to tell her how to come to Christ. "Just come to him as you are," Dr. Malan said. This she did, and went away rejoicing. Shortly afterwards she wrote this hymn, "Just as I am, without one plea."[28]

Christ has a way of using ordinary people to do amazing things that may bring hearts to Christ! Just listen for that still, small voice and act on it, just as you are! God knows who you are, so you too can come to Christ and say, "I come **Just As I Am**. May I be used by You, Lord!"

Prayer

Thank You, Lord, that no matter my condition or situation, if I come to You for salvation, You will in no wise cast me out. Then I may learn and be used by You, dear God.

Amen.

The Last Mile of the Way

1. If I walk in the path-way of du - ty, If I work till the
2. If for Christ I pro - claim the glad sto - ry, If I seek for His
3. And if here I have ear - nest - ly striv - en And have tried all His

close of the day, I shall see the great King in His beau - ty
sheep gone a - stray, I am sure He will show me His glo - ry
will to o - bey, 'Twill en - hance all the rap - ture of heav - en

Fine Chorus

When I've gone the last mile of the way. When I've gone the last mile

of the way, I will rest at the close of the
the last mile of the way, at the

D.S. al Fine

day And I know there are joys that a - wait me
close of the day,

The Last Mile of the Way

Lyrics by Johnson Oatman Jr. (1856–1922)
Music by William E. Marks (1872–1954)

For the wages of sin is death; but the gift of God
is eternal life through Jesus Christ our Lord.
(Romans 6:23)

We read this about Johnson Oatman Jr., written in 1914:

> Johnson Oatman, Jr., son of Johnson and Rachel Ann Oatman, was born near Medford, N. J., April 21, 1856. His father was an excellent singer, and it always delighted the son to sit by his side and hear him sing the songs of the church.
>
> …Mr. Oatman received his education at Herbert's Academy, Princetown, N. J., and the New Jersey Collegiate Institute, Bordentown, N. J. At the age of nineteen he joined the M.E. Church, and a few years later he was granted a license to preach the Gospel…
>
> For many years he was engaged with his father in the mercantile business at Lumberton, N. J., under the firm name of Johnson Oatman & Son…
>
> He has written over three thousand hymns, and no gospel song book is considered as being complete unless it contains some of his hymns. [By the end of his life he had written five thousand hymns.][29]

When reading about Johnson Oatman Jr. it seemed to me that he had the utmost respect for his father. This is how we should live—first respect ourselves, and this will help us to show respect for teachers, military, firefighters, police, pastors, always parents, and, most of all, God!

Prayer

Lord, we thank You that You teach us to be Your sons and daughters and to win others to Christ through the leading of the Holy Spirit, from our birth to the last mile of our way. Thank You, Lord.

Amen.

Leaning on the Everlasting Arms

1. What a fel-low-ship, what a joy di-vine, Lean-ing on the ev-er-last-ing arms;
2. Oh, how sweet to walk in this pil-grim way, Lean-ing on the ev-er-last-ing arms;
3. What have I to dread, what have I to fear, Lean-ing on the ev-er-last-ing arms?

What a bless-ed-ness, what a peace is mine, Lean-ing on the ev-er-last-ing arms.
O how bright the path grows from day to day, Lean-ing on the ev-er-last-ing arms.
I have bless-ed peace with my Lord so near, Lean-ing on the ev-er-last-ing arms.

Chorus

Lean - ing, lean - ing, Safe and se-cure from all a-larms;
Lean-ing on Je - sus, lean-ing on Je - sus,

Lean - ing, lean - ing, Lean-ing on the ev-er-last-ing arms.
Lean-ing on Je - sus, lean-ing on Je - sus,

Leaning on the Everlasting Arms

LYRICS BY ELISHA A. HOFFMAN (1839–1929)
MUSIC AND REFRAIN BY ANTHONY J. SHOWALTER (1858–1924)

The eternal God is thy refuge,
and underneath are the everlasting arms.
(Deuteronomy 33:27)

Mr. Anthony Showalter tells the story that as he returned to his boarding house room one day, he found two letters awaiting him from two former students whose wives had passed away. Showalter, desiring to comfort the men in the midst of their grief, wrote back. At the end of each letter, he included Deuteronomy 33:27 (above).

Robert Morgan writes, "He [Showalter] scribbled replies to his bereaved friends, then, reaching for another piece of paper, he wrote to his friend, hymnist Elisha Hoffman. 'Here is the chorus for a good hymn from Deuteronomy 33:27,' his letter said, 'but I can't come up with any verses.' Hoffman wrote three stanzas and sent them back. Showalter set it all to music, and ever since, these words have cheered us in adversity:

What have I to dread, what have I to fear,

Leaning on the everlasting arms.

I have blessed peace with my Lord so near,

Leaning on the everlasting arms."[30]

It seems that teamwork made this hymn. Are you a team player? Teamwork is sometimes difficult, but sometimes it is God's will to combine the talents of many people to create one extraordinary thing. Ask God to help you to work well with others, and keep the faith that you will rise to the challenge!

Prayer

Dear Lord, being good friends or marriage partners certainly takes teamwork. Most importantly, to fulfill Your plan, let us be sure that we are good teammates with You, Lord.

Amen.

Let the Lower Lights Be Burning

1. Bright - ly beams our Fa - ther's mer - cy From His light-house ev - er - more,
2. Dark the night of sin has set - tled, Loud the an - gry bil - lows roar;
3. Trim your fee - ble lamp, my broth - er! Some poor sail - or, tem - pest-tossed,

But to us He gives the keep - ing Of the lights a - long the shore.
Ea - ger eyes are watch - ing, long - ing For the lights a - long the shore.
Try - ing now to make the har - bor, In the dark - ness may be lost.

Chorus

Let the low - er lights be burn - ing, Send a gleam a - cross the wave!

Some poor faint - ing, strug - gling sea - man You may res - cue, you may save.

Let the Lower Lights Be Burning

LYRICS AND MUSIC BY PHILIP P. BLISS (1838–1876)

Ye are the light of the world. A city that is set on an hill cannot be hid. Neither do men light a candle, and put it under a bushel, but on a candlestick; and it giveth light unto all that are in the house. Let your light so shine before men, that they may see your good works, and glorify your Father which is in heaven.
(Matthew 5:14–16)

Philip P. Bliss directed music for the great nineteenth-century evangelist Rev. Dwight L. Moody. While listening to one of Moody's sermons, Bliss was inspired to write this hymn. Here is an excerpt from that moving Moody sermon:

A few years ago, at the mouth of Cleveland harbor there were two lights, one at each side of the bay, called the upper and lower lights; and to enter the harbor safely by night, vessels must sight both of the lights....

One wild, stormy night, a steamer was trying to make her way into the harbor. The Captain and pilot were anxiously watching for the lights.... "Do you see the lower lights?" "No," was the reply; "I fear we have passed them."

"Ah, there are the lights," said the pilot; "and they must be from the bluff on which they stand, the upper lights. We have passed the lower lights; and have lost our chance of getting into the harbor."...

The storm was so fearful that they could do nothing. They tried again to make for the harbor, but they went crash against the rocks, and sank to the bottom....

Christ himself is the upper light, and we are the lower lights, and the cry to us is, Keep the lower lights burning.... He will lead us safe to the sunlit shore of Canaan, where there is no more night.[31]

Prayer

Father, please keep us shining brightly, reflecting the glorious Light of the World. The Light came among us as flesh to give His life so that many people would be saved! Thank You, precious Jesus, that Your Word lights the way to salvation and eternal life!

Amen.

The Lily of the Valley

1. I have found a friend in Je-sus, He's ev-'ry-thing to me, He's the
2. O He all my grief has tak-en, and all my sor-rows borne; In temp-
3. He will nev-er, nev-er leave me, nor yet for-sake me here, While I

fair-est of ten-thou-sand to my soul; The Lil-y of the Val-ley, in
ta-tion He's my strong and might-y tow'r; I have all for Him for-sak-en, and
live by faith and do His bless-ed will; A wall of fire a-bout me, I've

Fine

Him a-lone I see All I need to cleanse and make me ful-ly whole.
all my i-dols torn From my heart, and now He keeps me by His pow'r.
noth-ing now to fear, With His man-na He my hun-gry soul shall fill.

D.S.— Bright and Morn-ing Star, He's the fair-est of ten-thou-sand to my soul.

In sor-row He's my com-fort, in trou-ble He's my stay, He
Tho' all the world for-sake me, and Sa-tan tempt me sore, Thru
Then sweep-ing up to glo-ry to see His bless-ed face, Where

D.S. al Fine

tells me ev-'ry care on Him to roll. He's the Lil-y of the Val-ley, the
Je-sus I shall safe-ly reach the goal. He's the Lil-y of the Val-ley, the
riv-ers of de-light shall ev-er roll. He's the Lil-y of the Val-ley, the

The Lily of the Valley

LYRICS BY CHARLES W. FRY (1838–1882)
MUSIC BY WILLIAM S. HAYS (1837–1907)

I am the rose of Sharon, and the lily of the valleys. As the lily among thorns, so is my love among the daughters. As the apple tree among the trees of the wood, so is my beloved among the sons.
I sat down under His shadow with great delight…. He brought me to the banqueting house, and His banner over me was love.
(Song of Solomon 2:1–4)

In 1881, inspired by the Song of Solomon, pictures formed in the heart and mind of Charles Fry. He penned a hymn about the intimate personal relationship he had with Jesus, which was all he needed "to cleanse and make [him] fully whole. In sorrow He's my comfort, in trouble He's my stay; He tells me every care on Him to roll."

In your life, you too can have a more intimate relationship with the Lord Jesus. The Bible says God's precious living Word, Jesus, is with you right now. He wants to speak through His Holy Spirit and through the Bible as you go through challenges like the death of a loved one, sickness, lack of a job, a child going through rehab, or lack of finances, food, or clothing for your family. Jesus knows what happens in this real world and wants to walk with you through whatever you are facing. He wants to give you wisdom and grow His character in you through all situations of your life.

Make this your prayer: *Lord, let me know You intimately throughout my life. May I gain an understanding of You, for You are the Word of God, who came to the earth and sacrificed Your miraculous life so we may have salvation and eternal life.*

Prayer

*Thank You, Jesus, for giving us beauty for ashes. You are the **Lily of the Valley**! What a fragrance of beauty You are, Lord. You, Father God, created the beauty on this earth so we may enjoy the flowers and foliage. While an earthly **Lily of the Valley** signifies happiness, purity, humility, and renewal, the heavenly **Lily of the Valley** brings us the gift of salvation and eternal life. Thank You, Lord Jesus.*

Amen.

Love Divine, All Loves Excelling

1. Love di - vine, all love ex - cel - ling, Joy of heav'n, to earth come down!
2. Breathe, O breathe Thy lov - ing Spir - it In - to ev - 'ry trou - bled breast;
3. Come, Al - might - y to de - liv - er, May we all Thy life re - ceive;
4. Fin - ish then Thy new cre - a - tion, Pure, un - spot - ted, may we be;

Fix in us thy hum - ble dwell - ing, All Thy faith - ful mer - cies crown;
May we all in Thee in - her - it; May we find the prom - ised rest;
Sud - den - ly re - turn, and nev - er, Nev - er - more thy tem - ples leave;
May we see our whole sal - va - tion Per - fect - ly se - cured by Thee;

Je - sus, Thou art all com - pas - sion, Pure, un - bound - ed love Thou art;
Take a - way the love of sin - ning, Take our load of guilt a - way;
Thee we would be al - ways bless - ing, Serve Thee as Thy hosts a - bove,
Changed from glo - ry in - to glo - ry, Till in heav'n we take our place,

Vis - it us with Thy sal - va - tion, En - ter ev - 'ry trem - bling heart!
End the work of Thy be - gin - ning, Bring us to e - ter - nal day.
Pray, and praise Thee, with - out ceas - ing, Glo - ry in Thy per - fect love.
Till we cast our crowns be - fore Thee, Lost in won - der, love and praise.

Love Divine, All Loves Excelling

LYRICS BY CHARLES WESLEY (1707–1788)
MUSIC BY JOHN ZUNDEL (1815–1882)

And to know the love of Christ, which passeth knowledge,
that ye might be filled with all the fulness of God.
(Ephesians 3:19)

Charles Wesley wrote many thousands of hymns during his life. He wrote many of them while on horseback as he went from one place of ministry to the next. "**Love Divine, All Loves Excelling**" is considered one of his greatest hymns, according to Julian's *Dictionary of Hymnology*.[32] This hymn invites Jesus to enter our hearts, making His dwelling place in us, taking away our desire to sin, and thus freeing us and giving us liberty to worship and praise Him.

"**Love Divine, All Loves Excelling**" was included in *Hymns for Those that Seek and Those that Have Redemption in the Blood of Jesus Christ*, of 1747. Are you one who already has redemption in the blood of Jesus Christ? Let the words of invitation in this hymn be your own words inviting Jesus to "come, Almighty to deliver," and to "finish then Thy new creation, pure and spotless let us be."

Only the transformative power of Jesus Christ can perfectly restore us in Him. By His grace and power we are

Changed from glory into glory,

Till in heaven we take our place,

Till we cast our crowns before Thee,

Lost in wonder, love, and praise.

What a beautiful day that will be, when we finally gaze upon the face of Him who saved us from the power of sin! But until then, let us sing this wonderful hymn as a prayer before the Lord.

Prayer

Holy Father, we know these blessings and gifts all come from You because of Your glorious, majestic power of **Love Divine**. *May we share what You have given to us with others that You send along our path. Thank You, Father.*

Amen.

Love Lifted Me

1. I was sink-ing deep in sin, Far from the peace-ful shore, Ver-y deep-ly
2. All my heart to Him I give, Ev-er to Him I'll cling, In His bless-ed
3. Souls in dan-ger, look a-bove, Je-sus com-plete-ly saves; He will lift you

stained with-in, Sink-ing to rise no more; But the Mas-ter of the sea
pres-ence live, Ev-er His prais-es sing. Love so might-y and so true
by His love Out of the an-gry waves. He's the Mas-ter of the sea,

Heard my de-spair-ing cry, From the wa-ters lift-ed me Now safe am I.
Mer-its my soul's best songs; Faith-ful, lov-ing ser-vice too, To Him be-longs.
Bil-lows His will o-bey; He your Sav-ior wants to be, Be saved to-day.

Chorus

Love lift-ed me! Love lift-ed me!
e-ven me! e-ven me!

1.
When noth-ing else could help, Love lift-ed me.
2.
Love lift-ed me.

112

Love Lifted Me

LYRICS BY JAMES ROWE (1865–1933)
MUSIC BY HOWARD E. SMITH (1863–1918)

There is no fear in love; but perfect love casteth out fear: because fear
hath torment. He that feareth is not made perfect in love.
(1 John 4:18)

For whatsoever is born of God overcometh the world:
and this is the victory that overcometh the world, even our faith.
(1 John 5:4)

James Rowe was born in Devonshire, England, on New Years Day, 1865. He is credited with publishing more than nine thousand hymns and other written works.

Rowe and Howard E. Smith worked closely together in the composition of this hymn, with Smith at the piano. Smith is described as having suffered from arthritis that terribly knotted his hands. Yet in spite of this infirmity, he was able to play and compose on the piano. When the two had finished their labors, the hymn "**Love Lifted Me**" was brought forth.

Jesus rises above all calamities, difficulties, and "angry waves" of life. Yet He does not leave us as "souls in danger," but bids us to "look above" and allow His loving arms to lift us into His presence.

Jesus, You came with a message of love and salvation. We know "God is love," and Your Word, the Bible, is the only sure and truthful voice we can trust. There is no error in Your Word or Your ways. We love and thank You, that Your love has lifted us out of the miry clay and set our feet on You, Jesus, the Rock. Thank You, Jesus, for Your love that lifts us every day.

"…Nor could the scroll contain the whole, Tho stretched from sky to sky," James Heath, 1800

The Love of God

LYRICS AND MUSIC BY FREDERICK M. LEHMAN (1868–1953)

A new commandment I give unto you, that ye love one another;
as I have loved you, that ye also love one another. By this shall all
men know that ye are My disciples, if ye have love one to another.
(John 13:34–35)

We read the fascinating tale of Lehman's hymn in Osbeck's *Amazing Grace*:

The unusual third stanza of the hymn was a small part of an ancient lengthy poem composed in 1096 by a Jewish songwriter, Rabbi Mayer, in Worms, Germany. The poem, entitled "Hadamut," was written in the Arabic language. The lines were found one day in revised form on the walls of a patient's room in an insane asylum after the patient's death. The opinion has since been that the unknown patient, during times of sanity, adapted from the Jewish poem what is now the third verse of "**The Love of God**."

The words of the third stanza were quoted one day at a Nazarene camp meeting. In the meetings was Frederick M. Lehman, a Nazarene pastor, who described his reaction:

"The profound depths of the lines moved us to preserve the words for future generations. Not until we had come to California did this urge find fulfillment, and that at a time when circumstances forced us to hard manual labor. One day, during short intervals of inattention to our work, we picked up a scrap of paper and added the first two stanzas and chorus to the existing third verse lines."

Pastor Lehman completed the hymn in 1917. His daughter Claudia (Mrs. W. W. Mays) assisted him with the music.[33]

Prayer

Lord, thank You for Your love toward us, for giving us the Ten Commandments for our instruction. We ask that You forgive the United States of America for rejecting Your laws and direction. Help us to replace Your love and law back into our lives, schools, communities, and hearts! May we be obedient to Your commands.

Amen.

The Love of God

1. The love of God is great - er far Than tongue or pen can ev - er tell; It goes be - yond the high - est star, And reach - es to the low - est hell; The guilt - y pair, bowed down with care, God gave His Son to win; His err - ing child He rec - on - ciled And par - doned from his sin.

2. When hoar - y time shall pass a - way, And earth - ly thrones and king - doms fall; When men who here re - fuse to pray, On rocks and hills and moun - tains call; God's love, so sure, shall still en - dure, All meas - ure - less and strong; Re - deem - ing grace to Ad - am's race The saints' and an - gels' song.

3. Could we with ink the o - cean fill, And were the skies of parch - ment made; Were ev - 'ry stalk on earth a quill, And ev - 'ry man a scribe by trade; To write the love of God a - bove Would drain the o - cean dry; Nor could the scroll con - tain the whole, Tho stretched from sky to sky.

The Love of God, continued

O love of God, how rich and pure! How meas - ure - less and strong!

It shall for ev - er - more en - dure The saints' and an - gels' song.

A Mighty Fortress Is Our God

1. A might-y for-tress is our God, A bul-wark nev-er fail - ing;
2. Did we in our own strength con - fide Our striv-ing would be los - ing;
3. And tho this world, with e - vil filled, Should threat-en to un - do us;

Our help-er He, a - mid the flood Of mor-tal ills pre - vail - ing.
Were not the right One on our side The Man of God's own choos - ing.
We will not fear, for God hath willed His truth to tri - umph thru us.

For still our an - cient foe Doth seek to work us woe; His craft and pow'r are
Dost ask who that may be? Christ Je - sus, it is He; Lord Sab - aoth is His
Let goods and kin - dred go, This mor-tal life al - so; The bod - y they may

great, And, armed with cru - el hate, On earth is not his e - - - qual.
name, From age to age the same, And He must win the bat - - - tle.
kill: God's truth a - bid - eth still, His king - dom is for - ev - - - er.

A Mighty Fortress Is Our God

Lyrics and Music by Martin Luther (1483–1546)
Translated by Frederick H. Hedge (1805–1890)

*There is a river, the streams whereof shall make glad the city of God,
the holy place of the tabernacles of the most High. God is in the
midst of her; she shall not be moved: God shall help her,
and that right early. The heathen raged, the kingdoms were moved:
He uttered His voice, the earth melted.
The Lord of hosts is with us; the God of Jacob is our refuge. Selah.*
(Psalm 46:4–7)

Martin Luther had many interests and talents. He pursued them and became successful in them. People remember his great work as a reformer, but among Luther's lesser-known pursuits was a love of poetry and music.

Robert Morgan writes, "There in his little Thuringian village, young Martin grew up listening to his mother sing. He joined a boys' choir that sang at weddings and funerals. He became proficient with the flute (recorder), and his volcanic emotions often erupted in song."[34]

Luther's most famous hymn is "**A Mighty Fortress Is Our God.**" Psalm 46:1 reminds us that, "*God is our refuge and strength, a very present help in trouble.*" In Jeremiah 16:19 we read, "*O Lord, my strength, and my fortress, and my refuge in the day of affliction.*"

As in Martin's life, God has given each of us talents to use in our lives to bring Him glory. God Almighty has given us all permission to use His Word. If we will individually take God's Word and line up our lives with God's commandments, we will find that He is our fortress and refuge in times of attack from the enemy. *Praise the Lord who gives us victory.*

Prayer

Dear Lord, our protector and fortress, when we need a place of safety we can call on You at any hour knowing that You, Almighty God, are our answer to every need.

Amen.

Moment by Moment

Moment by Moment

LYRICS BY D. W. WHITTLE (1840–1901)
MUSIC BY MAY WHITTLE MOODY (1870–1963)

Behold, I shew you a mystery; We shall not all sleep,
but we shall all be changed.
(1 Corinthians 15:51)

Growing up, Dad was the only boy in the midst of three older and three younger sisters. He and grandfather worked the land on the farm in Oklahoma. It was hard work and required many long hours, making men out of boys.

There was a terrible drought one particular year, and it was devastating to watch the crops die. On top of that, my grandfather was a smoker and chewed tobacco, and had developed a seriously alarming cough.

One night during this severe drought, Dad—at age nineteen—went out to cool off, lying on top of the cellar door. Looking up at the stars, he said, "God, if You are truly God, I need a miracle. I am asking You to bring rain to this area, to fill every low spot, soaking the ground to save our crops. I am also asking You to help my father quit smoking and chewing tobacco and heal his health from that cough! If You do this, I will never doubt You, but if You don't, I will never believe in You!"

My dad then went inside and laid his head on the open windowsill, falling asleep. When he awoke, it was to the sound of his father's voice saying, "Gertrude, I believe these cigarettes and tobacco are killing me. I'm never going to use them again. And would you just look—every low spot is filled with rainwater soaking the ground!" My dad was overjoyed that the crops would be saved!

Later, my father attended a revival where he asked the Lord Jesus to be his Savior. Dad immediately changed his lifestyle. He began reading the Bible, then preaching. He continued to preach for the next fifty-five years. My father's salvation experience and ministry have impacted many people's lives throughout the years. I pray that his story will strengthen your faith too!

Prayer

Father God, You heard and answered a young man's prayer. Thank You for the miracle that changed my father's life. Help us all to receive and acknowledge the miracles You provide each day of our lives.

Amen.

My Faith Looks Up to Thee

1. My faith looks up to Thee, Thou Lamb of Cal - va - ry,
2. May Thy rich grace im - part Strength to my faint - ing heart,
3. While life's dark maze I tread, And griefs a - round me spread,

Sav - ior di - vine; Now hear me while I pray; Take all my
My zeal in - spire; As Thou hast died for me, O may my
Be Thou my guide; Bid dark - ness turn to day, Wipe sor - row's

sins a - way; O let me from this day Be whol - ly Thine.
love to Thee, Pure warm, and change - less be, A liv - ing fire.
tears a - way, Nor let me ev - er stray From Thee a - side.

My Faith Looks Up to Thee

Lyrics by Ray Palmer (1808–1887)
Music by Lowell Mason (1792–1872)

Therefore being justified by faith, we have peace with God through our Lord Jesus Christ: By whom also we have access by faith into this grace wherein we stand, and rejoice in hope of the glory of God.
(Romans 5:1–2)

A mos R. Wells, author of *A Treasure of Hymns*, wrote of this hymn, "This is probably the greatest hymn written by an American." He quotes lyricist Ray Palmer as saying that "the words of the hymn…were born of my own soul." Wells goes on to relate the following incident connected with "**My Faith Looks Up to Thee**":

Eight young Christian soldiers…met for prayer in a tent just before one of the terrible battles of the Wilderness in the Civil War. They desired to write a statement which should show how they faced death and go as a comforting message to the relatives of those whom the coming battle might remove from earth. They decided to copy this hymn and sign it as their sufficient declaration of Christian faith, and they did so. On the morrow seven of those brave Union soldiers died for their country, and received in their own experience the blessed realization of the hymn's closing stanza:

> *When ends life's transient dream,*
> *When death's cold, sullen stream*
> *Shall o'er me roll,*
> *Blest Saviour, then, in love,*
> *Fear and distrust remove;*
> *O bear me safe above,*
> *A ransomed soul.*[35]

Prayer

Lord, we know if we are faithful, blessings will come to us, and a faithful servant will be abundantly supplied. So help us Lord, when we are tempted to be unfaithful. Give us strength to faithfully stand in obedience to You.

Amen.

My Hope Is Built on Nothing Less

1. My hope is built on noth-ing less Than Je-sus' blood and right-eous-ness;
2. When dark-ness veils His love-ly face, I rest on His un-chang-ing grace;
3. His oath, His cov-e-nant, His blood, Sup-port me in the whelm-ing flood;
4. When He shall come with trum-pet sound, O may I then in Him be found,

I dare not trust the sweet-est frame, But whol-ly lean on Je-sus' name.
In ev-'ry high and storm-y gale, My an-chor holds with-in the veil.
When all a-round my soul gives way, He then is all my hope and stay.
Dressed in His right-eous-ness a-lone, Fault-less to stand be-fore the throne.

Chorus

On Christ, the Sol-id Rock, I stand; All oth-er ground is sink-ing sand, All oth-er ground is sink-ing sand.

My Hope Is Built on Nothing Less

LYRICS BY REV. EDWARD MOTE (1797–1874)
MUSIC BY WILLIAM B. BRADBURY (1816–1868)

And he said, the LORD is my rock, and my fortress, and my deliverer.
(2 Samuel 22:2)

*Therefore whosoever heareth these sayings of Mine, and doeth them,
I will liken him unto a wise man, which built his house upon a rock.*
(Matthew 7:24)

One day, Edward Mote scribbled a verse on the way to work that came to his mind by inspiration of the Holy Spirit. A short time later, he went to visit a friend whose wife was ill. In Mote's own words, "He looked for his hymn-book but could find it nowhere. I said, 'I have some verses in my pocket; if he liked we would sing them.' We did; and his wife enjoyed them so much, that after service he asked me, as a favour, to leave a copy of them for his wife."[36]

But the fruit of the Spirit is love, joy, peace, longsuffering, gentleness, goodness, faith, meekness, temperance [self control]: *against such there is no law. And they that are Christ's have crucified the flesh with the affections and lusts.* (Galatians 5:22–24)

When we ask Jesus to become our Savior and to master our lives, a supernatural flow of the very characteristics of God come into our spirit through our teacher, the glorious Holy Spirit of God. As we grow and learn in and from God's Word, God's traits become our own traits, and begin to gush forth like mighty rushing water streaming in to protect and cleanse us from the inside out! So let the fruit of the Holy Spirit become a beautiful fragrance of God's love flowing out of you, to all in your path.

Prayer

Thank You, masterful Lord, that You are completely trustworthy and absolutely faithful to Your Word. Help us to develop the qualities of faithfulness and loyalty as we endeavor to live a life of integrity.

Amen.

My Jesus, I Love Thee

1. My Je - sus, I Love Thee, I know Thou art mine; For Thee all the
2. I love Thee, be - cause Thou has first loved me, And pur - chased my
3. In man - sions of glo - ry and end - less de - light, I'll ev - er a-

fol - lies of sin I re - sign; My gra - cious Re - deem - er, My
par - don on Cal - va - ry's tree; I love Thee for wear - ing The
dore Thee in heav - en so bright; I'll sing with the glit - te - ring

Sav - ior art Thou: If ev - er I loved Thee, my Je - sus, 'tis now.
thorns on Thy brow: If ev - er I loved Thee, my Je - sus, 'tis now.
crown on my brow: If ev - er I loved Thee, my Je - sus, 'tis now.

My Jesus, I Love Thee

LYRICS BY WILLIAM R. FEATHERSTONE (1846–1873)
MUSIC BY ADONIRAM JUDSON GORDON (1836–1895)

We love Him, because He first loved us…. And this commandment have we from Him, That he who loveth God love his brother also.
(1 John 4:19, 21)

A sixteen-year-old from Montreal wrote this hymn shortly after he experienced a Christian conversion. It should be an encouragement to all who are young, or young in their faith, as it expresses in beautiful verse the full glorious message of redemption found in Jesus.

The apostle Paul had a spiritual son, young Timothy, whom he referred to as *"my own son in the faith"* (1 Timothy 1:2). To Timothy Paul said, *"Let no man despise thy youth; but be thou an example of the believers, in word, in conversation, in charity, in spirit, in faith, in purity"* (1 Timothy 4:12).

Another Biblical example of a youth called to godly assignments far beyond his age is the Old Testament prophet, Jeremiah. When God called him, Jeremiah declared, *"Ah, Lord GOD! behold, I cannot speak: for I am a child."* But God assured Jeremiah, *"Say not, I am a child: for thou shalt go to all that I shall send thee, and whatsoever I command thee thou shalt speak"* (Jeremiah 1:6–7).

Some may be called by God in their elder years, and others while very young. God knows how best to use us, and he does not consider youth or old age an impediment to achieving His purposes. In fact, He often seems to choose the most unlikely people to accomplish His plans. So don't worry that you are too young or too old to serve God effectively. Think of young William Featherstone, who died at age twenty-six and only wrote one hymn so far as is known, but that hymn has been an ageless blessing.

Prayer

My Jesus, I Love Thee for saving my soul and making me whole. Thank You for helping me to live a clean life according to the Bible and directing me by the Holy Spirit's power that is supernatural, transcending all that is commonplace.

Amen.

Near the Cross

1. Je - sus, keep me near the cross; There a pre - cious foun - tain,
2. Near the cross, a trem - bling soul, Love and mer - cy found me;
3. Near the cross! O Lamb of God, Bring its scenes be - fore me;

Free to all, a heal - ing stream, Flows from Cal - v'ry's moun - tain.
There the bright and Morn - ing Star Sheds its beams a - round me.
Help me walk from day to day With its shad - ows o'er me.

Chorus

In the cross, in the cross, Be my glo - ry ev - er;

Till my rap - tured soul shall find Rest be - yond the riv - er.

Near the Cross

Lyrics by Fanny J. Crosby (1820–1915)
Music by William Howard Doane (1832–1915)

And He said to them all, If any man will come after Me,
let him deny himself, and take up his cross daily, and follow Me.
For whosoever will save his life shall lose it: but whosoever
will lose his life for My sake, the same shall save it.
(Luke 9:23–24)

Our enemy the devil is seeking a person filled with pride! "*Be sober, be vigilant; because your adversary the devil, as a roaring lion, walketh about, seeking whom he may devour: Whom resist stedfast in the faith, knowing that the same afflictions are accomplished in your brethren that are in the world*" (1 Peter 5:8–9).

Don't let the enemy blind you from seeing the consequence of bondage. "*The thief cometh not, but for to steal, and to kill, and to destroy: I am come that they might have life, and that they might have it more abundantly*" (John 10:10).

The Lord is fair, righteous, and just. It is only by faith that you can please God. God always has acted and always will act righteously toward you! God is faithful. Can you blindly trust people? We pray, "Lord please use me," but then we say, "Lord when they ask me to do this or that at church or when visiting someone, I just feel like I'm being used!"

Jesus spoke, "*Inasmuch as ye have done it unto one of the least of these My brethren, ye have done it unto Me*" (Matthew 25:40). Yes, be "used." Give your time, your money, your life, to Jesus, remembering that He gave His life for us—and say, "Jesus, keep me **Near the Cross**."

Prayer

Lord, I know that faith puts no pressure on people. I know that my job is not my source and all that I have has come from You, God. Philippians 4:19–20 says, "But my God shall supply all your need according to His riches in glory by Christ Jesus. Now unto God and our Father be glory for ever and ever. Amen."

Amen.

Nearer, My God, to Thee

1. Near - er, my God, to Thee, Near - er to Thee! E'en tho' it be a cross
2. Tho' like the wan - der - er, The sun gone down, Dark - ness be o - ver me,
3. There let the way ap - pear Steps un - to heav'n; All that Thou send - est me,
4. Or, if on joy - ful wing, Cleav - ing the sky, Sun, moon, and stars for - got,

D.S.— Near - er, my God, to Thee,

Fine   *D.S. al Fine*

That rais - eth me; Still all my song shall be, Near - er, my God, to Thee,
My rest a stone; Yet in my dreams I'd be Near - er, my God, to Thee,
In mer - cy giv'n; An - gels to beck - on me Near - er, my God, to Thee,
Up - ward I fly; Still all my song shall be, Near - er, my God, to Thee,

Near - er to Thee!

Jacob's ladder by Wenceslas Hollar, 1607–1677

130

Nearer, My God, to Thee

LYRICS BY SARAH FLOWER ADAMS (1805–1848)
MUSIC BY ELIZA ADAMS (1803–1846)

Know ye not that the unrighteous shall not inherit the kingdom of God? Be not deceived.... What? know ye not that your body is the temple of the Holy Ghost which is in you, which ye have of God, and ye are not your own? For ye are bought with a price: therefore glorify God in your body, and in your spirit, which are God's.
(1 Corinthians 6:9a, 19–20)

Sarah Flower Adams loved the stage and hoped to become an actress one day. However, her health was frail, so instead she focused her creativity on writing. Among her writings were hymns for which her sister Eliza often composed the music.

The story is told that Sarah and Eliza's pastor, William Johnson Fox, once shared with the sisters about his need for a hymn to go with an upcoming sermon on the subject of Jacob's ladder at Beth El, from Genesis 28. God blessed Sarah and Eliza with this beautiful hymn that filled the need of the moment.

We read in Wells's *Treasure of Hymns* the following touching story of mutual self-sacrifice:

Eliza, the elder sister, became weakened in caring for Sarah through a long illness, and Sarah's death, in turn, was hastened, doubtless, by her care for Eliza in her last sickness. The two passed away within a short interval, the elder in December, 1846, and Sarah on August 14, 1848. The hymns sung at both funerals were by Sarah, with music by Eliza.[37]

Each of us has a story. The one God writes for us may take us down unexpected paths. We need to always know there is a plan and purpose for what we experience. Take comfort in knowing you are never alone, but God Himself is transforming your life to fulfill His glorious plan.

Prayer

Lord, please change me and use me so that Your plan will miraculously show others their need for You to become Lord and Savior of their lives. Guide them into the fullness of Your power and grace.

Amen.

Nothing But the Blood

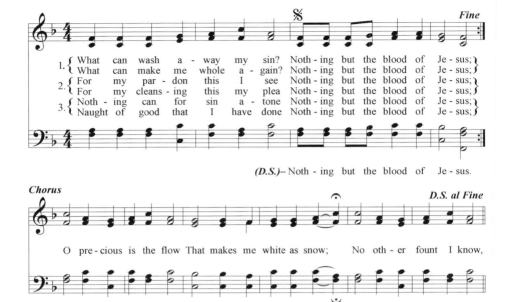

1. What can wash a - way my sin? Noth - ing but the blood of Je - sus;
   What can make me whole a - gain? Noth - ing but the blood of Je - sus;
2. For my par - don this I see Noth - ing but the blood of Je - sus;
   For my cleans - ing this my plea Noth - ing but the blood of Je - sus;
3. Noth - ing can for sin a - tone Noth - ing but the blood of Je - sus;
   Naught of good that I have done Noth - ing but the blood of Je - sus;

(D.S.)– Noth - ing but the blood of Je - sus.

Chorus

O pre - cious is the flow That makes me white as snow; No oth - er fount I know,

Nothing But the Blood

LYRICS AND MUSIC BY ROBERT LOWRY (1826–1899)

For this is My blood of the new testament, which is shed for many
for the remission of sins. But I say unto you,
I will not drink henceforth of this fruit of the vine, until that day
when I drink it new with you in My Father's kingdom.
(Matthew 26:28–29)

*L*owry is the composer of many familiar hymns, including "Shall We Gather at the River" and "My Life Flows on in Endless Song." He composed melodies for such lyricists as Fanny Crosby and Annie Hawks. We can get a delightful sense of his poetic nature not just by his lyrics, but even by reviewing the titles of his Sunday school hymn books. Who would not wish to sing from volumes with such titles as *Happy Voices, Bright Jewels, Pure Gold, Royal Diadem*, and *Fountain of Song*?

Robert Lowry was born in Philadelphia in 1826, and as hymn historian John Julian wrote in 1892, Lowry was educated at Lewisburg University:

> Having received ordination as a Baptist Minister, his first charge was at West Chester, Pennsylvania. From thence he passed to New York City, and then to Brooklyn, N.Y. In 1876 he was appointed Professor of Rhetoric in his University. On resigning his Professorship he undertook the charge of the 2nd Baptist Church, New Jersey. [38]

Respect wisdom and character. Age brings with it a more experienced, developed, and learned knowledge.

Prayer

Father, You have told us that "without shedding of blood there is no remission" of sin (Hebrews 9:22). Thank You for shedding Your blood so that we are saved from sin and redeemed. Praise God from whom all blessings flow!

Amen.

O That Will Be Glory

1. When all my la - bors and tri - als are o'er, And I am safe on that
2. When by the gift of His in - fi - nite grace, I am ac - cord - ed in
3. Friends will be there I have loved long a - go; Joy like a riv - er a-

beau - ti - ful shore, Just to be near the dear Lord I a - dore
heav - en a place, Just to be there and to look on His face
round me will flow; Yet just a smile from my Sav - ior I know

Chorus

Will thru the ag - es be glo - ry for me. Oh, that will be
Oh, that will

glo - ry for me, Glo - ry for me, glo - ry for me; When by His grace
be glo - ry for me, Glo - ry for me, glo - ry for me;

I shall look on His face, That will be glo - ry, be glo - ry for me.

O That Will Be Glory

LYRICS AND MUSIC BY CHARLES H. GABRIEL (1856–1932)

*That the trial of your faith, being much more precious than of gold
that perisheth, though it be tried with fire, might be found unto
praise and honour and glory at the appearing of Jesus Christ.*
(1 Peter 1:7)

I wonder if, like me, as young girls you women were looking for a fairy-tale prince, but after a date, you knew he was just an actor wrapped in tin foil, not your knight in shining armor. A true knight in shining armor is a genuine Christian man who puts God first and his wife and family next. Together you walk the path that God has for you!

My sweet and talented husband Dino is a true knight in shining armor. He was to be a stillborn baby, because of a fall his mother Helen had taken. Dino's grandmother Christina was a devout, praying woman. While praying for her daughter she had a vision that satan had a grip around Helen's waist. The enemy was trying to kill the child within her. Dino's grandmother said, "In the Name of Jesus, I rebuke you, satan!" Then she saw satan turn loose of Helen's waist, and she heard him run down five flights of stairs. That is just how real it was to her.

The next morning when she spoke to Helen, she told her to go to the Greek doctor, Dr. Papadopoulos. He said, "It is a miracle! Your baby is alive and well!" Sure enough, Dino was born alive and very much so because he started playing piano at three years of age. God spoke to his mother's heart as she peered through the door watching him pick out the song "At the Cross" that he had heard in church that morning. God said to her, "This is the talent I have given to your son, and he will evangelize throughout the world."

Dino is the sweetest, most loving and gracious man I have ever known. He is a giver in every sense of the word. He is faithful and true to God and His work. I thank God for using his life as he has through the years, and also for helping me to fulfill my heart's calling alongside Dino. When we meet the Lord, **O That Will Be Glory.**

Prayer

Thank You, Lord, for the opportunities You are giving to us so we may win others to the Kingdom of Heaven! We love You, Jesus.

Amen.

O Worship the King

1. O wor-ship the King, all glo-rious a-bove, And grate-ful-ly
2. Thy boun-ti-ful care, what tongue can re-cite? It breathes in the
3. Frail chil-dren of dust, and fee-ble as frail, In Thee do we

sing His won-der-ful love; Our Shield and De-fend-er, the
air, it shines in the light; It streams from the hills, it de-
trust, nor find Thee to fail; Thy mer-cies how ten-der! how

An-cient of Days, Pa-vil-ioned in splen-dor, and gird-ed with praise.
scends to the plain, And sweet-ly dis-tills in the dew and the rain.
firm to the end! Our Ma-ker, De-fend-er, Re-deem-er, and Friend!

O Worship the King

LYRICS BY SIR ROBERT GRANT (1779–1838)
MUSIC ATTRIBUTED TO JOHANN M. HAYDN (1737–1806)

I will sing unto the LORD as long as I live: I will sing praise to my God while I have my being. My meditation of Him shall be sweet: I will be glad in the LORD.
(Psalm 104:33–34)

Sir Robert Grant followed in his father's footsteps as a politician, both of the men serving as members of Parliament and serving in business and government in India. Ernest E. Ryden, in *The Story of Our Hymns* (1930), writes:

> Although he did not enter the service of the Church but engaged in secular pursuits, [Grant] was a deeply spiritual man and his hymns bear testimony of an earnest, confiding faith in Christ.... When we learn that the man who wrote [this hymn] was never engaged in religious pursuits, but that his whole life was crowded with arduous tasks and great responsibilities in filling high government positions, we have reason to marvel.... The language is chaste and exalted. The rhythm is faultless. The lines are chiseled as perfectly as a cameo. The imagery is almost startling in its grandeur.[39]

Grant was inspired by a study of Psalm 104 in the writing of this hymn. In reading about the One *"clothed with honour and majesty,"* Grant recognized the King of kings, to whose wonderful love grateful songs are due!

Prayer

Lord, we thank You for such a great man as Sir Robert Grant, who loved and served You throughout his life. We may not all have the chance to devote our lives to "religious pursuits," but, Lord, may we be as dedicated as Sir Robert, and exalt You as our King of kings.

Amen.

Oh, How I Love Jesus

1. There is a name I love to hear, I love to sing its worth;
2. It tells me of a Sav-ior's love, Who died to set me free;
3. It tells of One whose lov-ing heart Can feel my deep-est woe;

It sounds like mu-sic in my ear, The sweet-est name on earth.
It tells me of His pre-cious blood, The sin-ner's per-fect plea.
Who in each sor-row bears a part, That none can bear be-low.

Chorus

Oh, how I love Je-sus, Oh, how I love Je-sus,

Oh, how I love Je-sus, Be-cause He first loved me.

Oh, How I Love Jesus

LYRICS BY FREDERICK WHITFIELD (1829–1904)
MUSIC: AMERICAN MELODY

Herein is love, not that we loved God, but that He loved us,
and sent His Son to be the propitiation for our sins.
(1 John 4:10)

"Oh, How I Love Jesus" is a song that expresses both praise and love to Jesus, because He first loved us.

Frederick Whitfield was born on January 7, 1829, in England. He became a minister in the Church of England. He published more than thirty works of prose and verse before he died on September 13, 1904.

This song text first appeared in 1855 and had nine stanzas, although today we generally don't sing more than four of them. The verses of this hymn speak of all that is contained in the very name of our Savior: His love for us, His blood shed to set us free, His answer to our "sinner's perfect plea," and His heart that shares our burden of sorrow. All that, and more, is expressed whenever we utter the name "Jesus."

Jesus loved us enough to lay down His life for us (John 3:16). We know that the name of Jesus is like a sweet fragrance. As we read in one of the rarely used stanzas of this song,

This name shall shed its fragrance still

Along this thorny road,

Shall sweetly smooth the rugged hill

That leads me up to God.

Prayer

"Oh, How I love Jesus" is not just a song title to us, for, Jesus, we truly love You and we know You love us. Thank You for redeeming us and helping us through sorrow and joy on our way to heaven. Jesus, You are our all in all.

Amen.

The Old Rugged Cross

1. On a hill far a - way stood an old rug - ged cross, The em - blem of
2. O that old rug-ged cross, so de - spised by the world, Has a won - drous at -
3. In that old rug-ged cross, stained with blood so di - vine, A won - drous
4. To the old rug-ged cross I will ev - er be true, Its shame and re -

suf - fring and shame; And I love that old cross where the dear - est and best
trac - tion for me; For the dear Lamb of God left His glo - ry a - bove,
beau - ty I see; For 'twas on that old cross Je - sus suf - fered and died,
proach glad - ly bear; Then He'll call me some day to my home far a - way,

Chorus

For a world of lost sin - ners was slain.
To bear it to dark Cal - va - ry. So I'll cher - ish the old rug - ged
To par - don and sanc - ti - fy me. So I'll cher - ish the cross, the
Where His glo - ry for - ev - er I'll share.

cross, Till my tro - phies at last I lay down; I will cling to the
old rug - ged cross,

old rug - ged cross, And ex - change it some day for a crown.
cross, the old rug - ged cross,

The Old Rugged Cross

LYRICS AND MUSIC BY GEORGE BENNARD (1873–1958)

But God forbid that I should glory, save in the cross of our Lord Jesus Christ, by whom the world is crucified unto me, and I unto the world.
(Galatians 6:14)

George Bennard was born into a coal-mining family in Youngstown, Ohio. His father died when he was sixteen years old, and soon after, George experienced salvation in Christ. He served with the Salvation Army, and became involved with the holiness movement of the time, which was rooted in Wesleyan Methodism.

The Old Rugged Cross was birthed from a tribulation in George's life that brought him great suffering, leading him to identify with the suffering of Christ and bringing a heightened awareness of the cross where Jesus' suffering occurred.[40]

Here are George Bennard's own words about the writing of this hymn:

> The inspiration came to me one day in 1913, when I was staying in Albion, Michigan. I began to write "**The Old Rugged Cross.**" I composed the melody first. The words that I first wrote were imperfect. The words of the finished hymn were put into my heart in answer to my own need. Shortly thereafter it was introduced at special meetings in Pokagon, Michigan, on June 7, 1913. The first occasion where it was heard outside of the church at Pokagon was at the Chicago Evangelistic Institute. There it was introduced before a large convention and soon it became extremely popular throughout the country.[41]

George Bennard's life was dedicated to Christ Jesus. Our Lord poured through him words that come from the revelation of God's Word, the Bible, to enlighten the people of God through song.

Prayer

Father God, fill our hearts with love. May we accept the light of Your love so that we can receive increase in understanding of You and Your Word, and share it with others.

Amen.

On Jordan's Stormy Banks

1. On Jordan's storm-y banks I stand, And cast a wish-ful eye,
2. O'er all those wide ex-tend-ed plains Shines one e-ter-nal day,
3. When shall I reach that hap-py place, And be for-ev-er blest?

To Ca-naan's fair and hap-py land, Where my pos-ses-sions lie.
There God the Son for-ev-er reigns And scat-ters night a-way.
When shall I see the Fa-ther's face, And in His bos-om rest?

Chorus

I am bound for the prom-ised land, I am bound for the prom-ised land;
prom-ised land,

Oh, who will come and go with me? I am bound for the prom-ised land.

On Jordan's Stormy Banks

Lyrics by Samuel Stennett (1727–1795)
Music: American Folk Hymn

For to me to live is Christ, and to die is gain.
(Philippians 1:21)

*And I saw no temple therein: for the Lord God Almighty and the
Lamb are the temple of it. And the city had no need of the sun,
neither of the moon, to shine in it: for the glory of God did lighten it,
and the Lamb is the light thereof.*
(Revelation 21:22–23)

Dino and I were in Israel recently. Israel is so exciting—just to be able to walk where Jesus walked, and see the olive trees, remembering that Jesus asked the disciples to pray with Him there just one hour. But their flesh was weak, so they fell asleep. As He prayed, Jesus sweat, as it were, drops of blood, as He knew the suffering that was to come. Yet He said, *"Not my will, but Thine, be done"* (Luke 22:42).

Dino and I viewed the hill of Golgotha, where our precious Lord Jesus, King of the Jews, was crucified. By the shed blood of the Lamb who went to the cross and suffered, we were healed and forgiven. We can use our faith and be whole, the Bible says. We viewed the tomb where Christ Jesus was buried but arose on the third day! He ascended to heaven to sit at the right hand of the Father. Now we await our soon-coming King.

Many signs of His return have been fulfilled. If He doesn't come before we go, then we will rise to meet Him in the air in the twinkling of an eye and will live with Him forever. Until then, we can stand **On Jordan's Stormy Banks**, as I did in Israel. I put my hands and feet into the water where John the Baptist baptized our Lord, and where from heaven came the Holy Spirit in the form of a dove. God Almighty spoke then, saying, *"This is my beloved Son, in whom I am well pleased"* (Matthew 3:17).

Prayer

Thank You, Lord, for the Word of God, which is Jesus, who came to earth for us and now intercedes for us before the Father. We praise You, Jesus—for our guide, the Holy Spirit, continually shows us the straight and narrow path to heaven. So until we get there, On Jordan's Stormy Banks we stand "and cast a wishful eye."

Amen.

The Empty Tomb
(Phillip Medhurst Collection of Bible illustrations in the possession of Revd. Philip De Vere, PD)

One Day!

Lyrics by J. Wilbur Chapman (1859–1918)
Music by Charles H. Marsh (1840–1867)

The Lord is my light and my salvation; whom shall I fear?
The Lord is the strength of my life; of whom shall I be afraid?
(Psalm 27:1)

One Day, to fulfill God's plan, we were born into this life. **One Day** each year we celebrate our birthday. **One Day** we heard of Jesus, God's only Son, and His love, death, and resurrection. **One Day** we said yes to salvation, and all things became new. We believed Jesus. Our example is He; our Redeemer is He; Our Savior is He; our Lord evermore; this Jesus is mine—O glorious day!

I vividly recall my salvation experience, which occurred **One Day** in my Sunday school class. I accepted Jesus as my Savior. Our teacher, Mother Anderson, who was so loving, explained clearly how much Jesus loves us, and how He will never leave or forsake us. We just commit our heart to Jesus and learn how to become obedient to Him. We heard that He had a perfect plan for our lives, with great blessing and a home in heaven with Jesus where there is no more time—just everlasting life. But until that day, we await His coming. "One day He's coming, oh, glorious day!"

We know that in **One Day** our lives can change direction, and even our nation can change direction. The way to get our nation back on its feet is to get on our knees.

One Day, when we accepted Jesus as our Savior, everything in our life became new, and we were changed. We will change again **One Day** in the twinkling of an eye, as we are caught up to meet Jesus in the air and go on to heaven to see our loved ones who have gone before us. Then we will live with God our Father forevermore.

*Thank You, our glorious Savior, that we can look forward to that **One Day** when we will live with You forevermore. We love You, Jesus.*

One Day!

One Day!, *continued*

Open My Eyes, That I May See

1. O - pen my eyes, that I may see Glimps - es of truth Thou hast for me;
2. O - pen my ears, that I may hear Thy word of truth Thou send - est clear;
3. O - pen my mouth, and let me bear Glad - ly the warm truth ev - 'ry - where;

Place in my hands the won - der - ful key That shall un - clasp, and
And while the wave - notes fall on my ear, Ev - 'ry - thing false will
O - pen my heart, and let me pre - pare Love with Thy chil - dren

Chorus

set me free. Si - lent - ly now I wait for Thee, Read - y, my God, Thy
dis - ap - pear. Si - lent - ly now I wait for Thee, Read - y, my God, Thy
thus to share. Si - lent - ly now I wait for Thee, Read - y, my God, Thy

will to see: O - pen my eyes, il - lu - mine me, Sav - ior Di - vine!
will to see: O - pen my ears, il - lu - mine me, Sav - ior Di - vine!
will to see: O - pen my heart, il - lu - mine me, Sav - ior Di - vine!

Open My Eyes, That I May See

LYRICS AND MUSIC BY CLARA H. SCOTT (1841–1897)

*Nevertheless,… the [veil] shall be taken away. Now the Lord is that
Spirit: and where the Spirit of the Lord is, there is liberty.
But we all, with open face beholding as in a glass the glory of the
Lord, are changed into the same image from glory to glory,
even as by the Spirit of the Lord.*
(2 Corinthians 3:16–18)

We need to keep God's holy Word in our heart and mind daily. When things seem rough on the job, quote one or two Scriptures to yourself. You will begin, as you do this, to feel the peaceful spirit inside that you desire. The Spirit of God and the Word of God will help you to *not* want to retort, or be sharp or angry back at one who may be treating you unfairly. You may want to immediately ask the Lord for supernatural power to overcome your circumstance.

We must give Jesus, who is the Word, and the Holy Spirit, who is our teacher, first place in our hearts. Even through the most difficult situations, like abuse, or the loss of a precious child or parent you love so much, or loss of your job, we must meditate on God's Word to find supernatural help. In those times, cherish the miracle-working stories that are in God's Word. You will find power to face the day with peace in your heart. Wait on God's answer. Don't act from your flesh, but give love to all. Judge none, because judging is God's job. Give gifts to those in need, and go to church, where you will enjoy the presence of the Lord in corporate worship.

*And Moses called unto all Israel, and said unto them, Ye have seen
all that the LORD did before your eyes in the land of Egypt unto
Pharaoh, and unto all his servants, and unto all his land…. Keep
therefore the words of this covenant, and do them, that ye may
prosper in all that ye do.* (Deuteronomy 29:2, 9)

Prayer

Lord God, our Father, please **Open My Eyes, That I May See,** *with
Your love and power to overcome any situation of my life. Through
Your supernatural joy we have the victory.*

Amen.

Praise Him! Praise Him!

1. Praise Him! Praise Him! Je-sus, our bless-ed Re-deem-er! Sing, O Earth, His wonder-ful love pro-claim! Hail Him! Hail Him! High-est arch-an-gels in glo-ry; Strength and hon-or give to His ho-ly Name! Like a shep-herd, Jesus will guard His child-ren, In His arms He car-ries them all day long;

2. Praise Him! Praise Him! Je-sus, our bless-ed Re-deem-er! For our sins He suf-fered, and bled, and died. He our Rock, our hope of e-ter-nal sal-va-tion; Hail Him! Hail Him! Je-sus the Cru-ci-fied. Sound His prais-es! Jesus who bore our sor-rows, Love un-bound-ed, won-der-ful, deep and strong;

3. Praise Him! Praise Him! Je-sus, our bless-ed Re-deem-er! Heav'n-ly por-tals loud with hos-an-nas ring! Je-sus, Sav-ior, liv-eth for-ev-er and ev-er. Crown Him! Crown Him! Proph-et, and Priest, and King! Christ is com-ing! O-ver the world vic-to-rious, Pow'r and glo-ry un-to the Lord be-long;

D.S.—Praise Him! Praise Him! tell of His ex-cel-lent great-ness; Praise Him! Praise Him! ev-er in joy-ful song!

Praise Him! Praise Him!

LYRICS BY FANNY J. CROSBY (1820–1915)
MUSIC BY CHESTER G. ALLEN (1838–1878)

*By Him therefore let us offer the sacrifice of praise to God
continually, that is, the fruit of our lips giving thanks to His name.*
(Hebrews 13:15)

*Because Thy lovingkindness is better than life,
my lips shall praise Thee.*
(Psalm 63:3)

God has honored us with so many things: His presence, health, wealth, family, and belongings. God has honored us with His presence by abiding in our midst. I praise Him for all He has blessed us with, knowing that God blesses us according to how we see, hear, speak, seek, and treat Him.

God doesn't need anything from us, but He knows exactly what we need: as Fanny writes in this hymn, "Love unbounded, wonderful, deep and strong."

How we speak about God's children honors or dishonors Him. Take this literally. Love for God is shown in love for other people. If we are unkind to God's children, we are unkind to Him. Furthermore, as those who call ourselves Christians, our ill-treatment of others reflects poorly on Him as well as Christians in general. Do not let your own words undermine your role as representative of God. We serve God through honoring, rather than judging, others. Do not allow the actions of others to cause you to disrespect Father God. This means we must also respect His children whom He has put in authority over us, such as our parents, bosses, pastors, police, firefighters, and political leaders. In this way, we, with clean hearts, can **Praise Him! Praise Him!** Jesus, our blessed Redeemer!

Prayer

Heavenly Father, may our hearts sing praise to You morning, noon, and night. May nothing of this life distract us from giving praise and honor continually to You, Lord.

Amen.

Precious Memories

1. Pre - cious mem - 'ries, un - seen an - gels, Sent from some - where to my soul;
2. Pre - cious fa - ther, lov - ing moth - er, Fly a - cross the lone - ly years;
3. As I trav - el on life's path - way, Know not what the years may hold;

How they lin - ger, ev - er near me, And the sa - cred past un - fold.
And old home scenes of my child - hood, In fond mem - o - ry ap - pear.
As I pon - der, hope grows fond - er, Pre - cious mem - 'ries flood my soul.

Chorus

Pre - cious mem - 'ries, how they lin - ger, How they ev - er flood my soul.

In the still - ness of the mid - night, Pre - cious sa - cred scenes un - fold.

Precious Memories

Lyrics and Music by John B. F. Wright (1877–1959)

Verily, verily, I say unto you, He that heareth My Word, and believeth on Him that sent Me, hath everlasting life, and shall not come into condemnation; but is passed from death unto life.
(John 5:24)

My life began with my mother's nurturing kisses and hugs. Then came tutoring and great friendship when I was a young teenager. But when I was sixteen my mom became extremely ill and almost died. After radical surgery, she did live but was never quite the same again. She became so dedicated to her health that I missed much fun between us. The time eventually came for me to make a change in my thinking, to mature and help in caring for and watching over her.

My mother was just twelve when she was saved at an arbor revival meeting, but her family was not saved. She began to minister with the only Bible she had, which did not have the books of Genesis or Revelation. That didn't matter! She was known as Oklahoma's "Indian girl preacher." Many people were saved under her ministry and transformed by God's Word. Her dad was not saved until just before he passed away, but he gladly drove her out to speak and back home, sometimes late in the night, for school the next day. He patched tires and struggled to find fuel on those trips, but always happily encouraged his little girl Helen. My mother truly loved God, studied the Bible intensely, and was an exciting teacher of Sunday Bible class.

At the close of mother's life, she lay still in bed for about three days. I put one earbud in her ear and the other in mine to listen to the Bible, as she was transitioning toward heaven. Suddenly, her eyes opened, looking straight upward. I asked, "Mom, do you see angels?" She mouthed, "I see Jesus, I see Jesus!" I then said, "Mom, if He is bidding you to come, go to Him. We are fine here, for He is taking care of us all. We will see you soon up there." She closed her eyes and in just moments she went to her eternal home, where I will see her soon, and we will rejoice together as we praise the Lord God! What a glorious home going.

Prayer

*Lord, as we recall **Precious Memories**, they linger on as we await our eternal home. Thank You for our parents, who are also Your children.*

Amen.

Redeemed

1. Re-deemed how I love to pro-claim it! Re-deemed by the blood of the Lamb;
2. Re-deemed and so hap-py in Je - sus, No lan-guage my rap-ture can tell;
3. I know I shall see in His beau-ty The King in whose law I de-light;

Re-deemed thru His in - fi - nite mer - cy, His child, and for - ev - er I am.
I know that the light of His pres-ence With me doth con - tin - ual - ly dwell.
Who lov - ing - ly guard-eth my foot-steps, And giv - eth me songs in the night.

Chorus

Re-deemed, re-deemed, Re-deemed by the blood of the Lamb;
re-deemed, re-deemed,

Re - deemed, re - deemed, His child, and for - ev - er, I am.
re-deemed, re-deemed,

Redeemed

LYRICS BY FANNY J. CROSBY (1820–1915)
MUSIC BY WILLIAM J. KIRKPATRICK (1838–1921)

O give thanks unto the LORD, for He is good:
for His mercy endureth for ever.
Let the redeemed of the LORD say so.
(Psalm 107:1–2)

The word *redeem* has a meaning in the context of the slave trade. Imagine that you are a slave—one whose life is not your own—standing on the auction block. Instead of being sold to a harsh new master for hard labor, someone comes along and buys you, only to hand you your freedom. In other words, he *redeems* you. How would you feel toward that person? Wouldn't you be overwhelmed with gratitude for his generosity that purchased your freedom? You might be so grateful, in fact, that you decide to devote yourself entirely to serving this one who bought you out of slavery.

This is exactly the situation we are in. Separated from God by our sin, we have become slaves of the enemy of God. But One came along and purchased our redemption. That One is Jesus Christ, and He bought us with His pure blood. We are no longer subject to the wrath of God that we fully deserve. Those of us who have received this precious gift can't help but live a life of gratitude to God Almighty, and proclaim, as Fanny writes:

Redeemed, how I love to proclaim it,

redeemed by the blood of the Lamb.

Go forth each day living life on purpose. Love all, judge none, serve others, and only worship One. We can celebrate our redemption every day, gained at the cost of our Savior's blood. "His child...forever, I am."

Prayer

Thank You, Jesus. Thank You so much for giving Your life to redeem us from sin, so that we may have eternal life.

Amen.

Revive Us Again

1. We praise Thee, O God, for the Son of Thy love, For Je - sus who
2. We praise Thee, O God, for Thy Spir - it of light, Who has shown us our
3. All glo - ry and praise to the Lamb that was slain, Who has borne all our
4. All glo - ry and praise to the God of all grace, Who has bought us and
5. Re - vive us a - gain; fill each heart with Thy love; May each soul be re -

Chorus

died, and is now gone a - bove.
Sav - ior, and scat - tered our night.
sins, and has cleansed ev - 'ry stain. Hal - le - lu - jah! Thine the glo - ry, Hal - le -
sought us and guid - ed our ways.
kin - dled with fire from a - bove.

lu - jah! A - men! Hal - le - lu - jah! Thine the glo - ry; Re - vive us a - gain.

Revive Us Again

LYRICS BY WILLIAM PATON MACKAY (1839–1885)
MUSIC BY JOHN J. HUSBAND (1760–1825)

But rejoice, inasmuch as ye are partakers of Christ's sufferings;
that, when His glory shall be revealed,
ye may be glad also with exceeding joy.
(1 Peter 4:13)

Rejoice in the Lord alway: and again I say, Rejoice.
(Philippians 4:4)

The story is told that William Paton Mackay was born to a godly Scottish mother who daily instilled Biblical principles into her son's life, though he did everything he could to reject her influences. When Mackay left for medical school his mother handed him a Bible with his name and John 3:16 inscribed inside.

At college Mackay lived a wicked life, drinking and enjoying the company of godless men. He cared so little for the gift his mother had given him that he pawned it.

When Mackay became a doctor he had occasion to treat a dying man who had no hope of recovery. This man had a peaceful countenance, though he had one request. He wanted to pay what was owed to his landlady, and he wished for her to bring him *his book*. Sadly, he died before these requests could be fulfilled.

Dr. Mackay visited the man's landlady and looked for the book he had asked for. By God's providence, it turned out to be the very Bible Mackay's mother had given him! He opened its cover and read at length the words his mother had written, as well as the Scriptures she had highlighted for his benefit. When he emerged from his readings, he was a changed man. From that moment, he left the medical field and devoted himself to ministry.

Prayer

Lord, I have heard the news about You. I am amazed at what You have done. Lord, do great things once again in our time, as You have done in the past. Lord, will You revive us again when we have sorrowing times, and bring back the joy of the Lord that is strength to our lives? Thank You for loving us. We praise You, Lord.

Amen.

Rock of Ages

1. Rock of Ag - es, cleft for me, Let me hide my - self in Thee;
2. Could my tears for - ev - er flow, Could my zeal no lan - guor know,
3. While I draw this fleet - ing breath, When my eyes shall close in death,

Let the wa - ter and the blood, From Thy wound - ed side which flowed,
These for sin could not a - tone; Thou must save, and Thou a - lone:
When I soar to worlds un - known, And be - hold Thee on Thy throne,

Be of sin the dou - ble cure, Save from wrath and make me pure.
In my hand no price I bring, Sim - ply to Thy cross I cling.
Rock of Ag - es, cleft for me, Let me hide my - self in Thee.

Rock of Ages

Lyrics by Rev. Augustus Montague Toplady (1740–1778)
Music by Thomas Hastings (1784–1872)

For who is God, save the Lord? and who is a rock, save our God?
(2 Samuel 22:32)

But the Lord is my defence; and my God is the Rock of my refuge.
(Psalm 94:22)

Rev. Augustus Montague Toplady was a contemporary of the Methodist preacher John Wesley, whom he famously and vociferously criticized on matters of theology. Wesley believed in and taught in his Methodism the perfectibility of man as part of the process of Christian sanctification. Interestingly, Toplady was converted under Methodist preaching, but he did not hold to its theology and instead became staunchly Calvinistic.

To counter Wesley, in the hymn "**Rock of Ages**" Toplady emphasizes "the water and the blood" from Christ's "riven side," lest it be forgotten that Jesus' works—not ours—are responsible for our sanctification.

God is often described in Scripture as a rock. Just as a large rock is strong and provides a hiding place, so God is strong and protects us from our enemies. *Rock of Ages* refers to Jesus, making a connection between the smitten rock of Numbers 20:8–11 in the Old Testament and Jesus' beaten body.

The story is told that Toplady was once caught in a sudden furious thunderstorm, and that he took shelter among massive rocks. It was in the shelter of those rocks that he is said to have composed this hymn.

Prayer

Lord, teach us how to examine our thoughts. Purify us in heart, mind, and spirit. Correct what needs to become pure and holy before You, God of heaven. Lord, let us be cleansed before You. Thank You, Father God.

Amen.

Shall We Gather at the River

1. Shall we gath-er at the riv-er, Where bright an-gel feet have trod,
2. On the mar-gin of the riv-er, Wash-ing up its sil-ver spray,
3. Ere we reach the shin-ing riv-er, Lay we ev-'ry bur-den down;
4. Soon we'll reach the sil-ver riv-er, Soon our pil-grim-age will cease;

With its crys-tal tide for-ev-er Flow-ing by the throne of God?
We will talk and wor-ship ev-er, All the hap-py, gold-en day.
Grace our spir-its will de-liv-er, And pro-vide a robe and crown.
Soon our hap-py hearts will quiv-er With the mel-o-dy of grace.

Chorus

Yes, we'll gath-er at the riv-er, The beau-ti-ful, the beau-ti-ful riv-er,

Gath-er with the saints at the riv-er, That flows by the throne of God.

160

Shall We Gather at the River

LYRICS AND MUSIC BY ROBERT LOWRY (1826–1899)

*Then cometh Jesus from Galilee to Jordan unto John, to be baptized
of him.… And Jesus, when He was baptized, went up straightway
out of the water: and, lo, the heavens were opened unto Him,
and He saw the Spirit of God descending like a dove,
and lighting upon Him: And lo a voice from heaven, saying,
This is My beloved Son, in whom I am well pleased.*
(Matthew 3:13, 16–17)

Robert Lowry was born March 12, 1826, in Philadelphia. As a youth, he was a member of the First Baptist Church of Philadelphia, where he taught Sunday school. After excelling in his schooling, he was ordained as a Baptist minister and pastored for forty-five years. Lowry is best known as a composer of many famous hymns, including "Nothing But the Blood" and "I Need Thee Every Hour."

In Rev. E. M. Long's *Illustrated History of Hymns and Their Authors*, we read about a time when Lowry was thinking of an epidemic that was then sweeping through New York. At that time, he contemplated that great reunion at the River of Life in heaven and the gathering of the saints before the Throne of God and the Lamb.

> All around friends and acquaintances were passing away.… "Seating myself at the organ," says [Lowry], "simply to give vent to the pent up emotions of the heart, the words and music of the hymn began to flow out, as if by inspiration:
> 'Shall we gather at the river, where bright angel feet have trod?'"[42]

Even out of our deepest loss God can comfort and encourage through His children in this world. Can God use you to be an encouragement to those suffering loss and to glorify Himself?

Prayer

We worship, You, Lord, and are grateful for the privilege of expressing Your comfort to others in this life. Our gifts come straight from You, Lord. Please anoint us to share the gift of the Word of God in the world. Thank You, Lord.

Amen.

Since I Have Been Redeemed

1. I have a song I love to sing,
2. I have a Christ who sat-is-fies, Since I have been re-deemed,
3. I have a home pre-pared for me,

Of my Re-deem-er, Sav-ior King,
To do His will my high-est prize, Since I have been re-deemed.
Where I shall dwell e-ter-nal-ly,

Chorus

Since I have been re-deemed, Since I have been re-
Since I have been re-deemed, Since I have been re-deemed,

deemed, I will glo-ry in His name; Since I have been re-
Since I have been re-deemed, Since

deemed, I will glo-ry in my Sav-ior's name.
I have been re-deemed,

Since I Have Been Redeemed

LYRICS AND MUSIC BY EDWIN O. EXCELL (1851–1921)

To redeem them that were under the law, that we might receive the adoptions of sons. And because ye are sons, God hath sent forth the Spirit of His Son into your hearts, crying, Abba, Father. Wherefore thou art no more a servant, but a son; and if a son, then an heir of God through Christ.
(Galatians 4:5–7)

The book of Ruth is a great book of the Bible to read. It tells a story of redemption, hope, and loyalty. Naomi's family moves to Moab from Bethlehem because of a famine. After settling, Naomi's husband Elimelech dies, leaving her alone with her sons, Mahlon and Chilion. The sons take wives of two Moabite women, Orpah and Ruth, but after ten years, both sons die as well. Naomi wishes to return to her homeland, and she implores Orpah and Ruth to return to their mothers' houses, since she cannot care for them.

Orpah departs, but Ruth clings to Naomi, uttering these famous words: "*Whither thou goest, I will go; and where thou lodgest, I will lodge: thy people shall be my people, and thy God my God*" (Ruth 1:16).

As Naomi and Ruth reach Bethlehem, it is the beginning of the barley harvest, so Naomi sends Ruth to follow the reapers in her kinsman Boaz's field. Boaz shows Ruth great tenderness and generosity because of Ruth's reputation as a virtuous woman.

In these days, a widow could be married off to a cousin or brother of the deceased husband. That person was called the "kinsman redeemer." One other cousin of Naomi's besides Boaz has the first right of refusal to marry Ruth, but he is not interested in her. God clears the way so that Boaz can wed Ruth, and they are blessed with a son, Obed. "*And Naomi took the child, and laid it in her bosom, and became nurse unto it*" (Ruth 4:16).

Many generations later, from that lineage of Ruth and her kinsman redeemer Boaz comes King David, and finally our Redeemer Jesus.

Prayer

Thank You, Lord, for Your redeeming love for us, and for this wonderful Biblical love story picturing how You are our Kinsman Redeemer!

Amen.

Softly and Tenderly

1. Soft - ly and ten - der - ly Je - sus is call - ing, Call - ing for you and for me;
2. Why should we tar - ry when Je - sus is plead - ing, Plead - ing for you and for me?
3. Time is now fleet - ing, the mo - ments are pass - ing, Pass - ing from you and from me;
4. Oh! for the won - der - ful love He has prom - ised, Prom - ised for you and for me;

See, on the por - tals He's wait - ing and watch - ing, Watch - ing for you and for me.
Why should we lin - ger and heed not His mer - cies, Mer - cies for you and for me?
Sha - ows are gath - er - ing, death warn - ings com - ing, Come - ing for you and for me.
Tho' we have sinned, He has mer - cy and par - don, Par - don for you and for me.

Chorus

Come home, come home, Ye who are wea - ry, come home;
Come home, come home,

Ear - nest - ly, ten - der - ly, Je - sus is call - ing, Call - ing, O sin - ner, come home!

Softly and Tenderly

LYRICS AND MUSIC BY WILL LAMARTINE THOMPSON (1847–1909)

Who His own self bare our sins in His own body on the tree,
that we, being dead to sins, should live unto righteousness:
by whose stripes ye were healed.
(1 Peter 2:24)

Will Thompson was born in East Liverpool, Ohio. When Will sent some of his songs to a commercial publisher for consideration, he was offered such a small amount for his work that he declined the offer. He didn't believe it to be a fair price for his music! Instead, he established a music publishing company of his own. He also opened a music store where he marketed his own music. He experienced such success in this endeavor that he became well known as the "bard of Ohio." One of his best-selling songs was a secular tune called "Gathering Seashells on the Seashore," which he wrote in ten minutes. That song sold 246,000 copies.

As a Christian, Thompson also wrote and promoted Christian music. He wrote "**Softly and Tenderly Jesus Is Calling**" in 1880, and famous evangelist Dwight L. Moody used it as an invitational song at his meetings. Thompson visited Moody's bedside in his last moments of life, and Mr. Moody confessed to Will, "I would rather have written '**Softy and Tenderly Jesus is Calling**' than anything I have been able to do in my life." What a rich blessing to receive from one who was such a great witness for Christ![43]

Thompson used to carry a piano on a horse-drawn wagon and travel to rural areas of Ohio to share his musical gifts with those who rarely got the opportunity to hear music. In many creative ways he gave his life to serve God and gave much to others. When we give what belongs to God in tithes, which is ten percent, we then need to ask God what more to give, listening to God as to how to bless others.

Prayer

*Dear God, help us to hear Jesus **Softly and Tenderly** calling as we listen to hear His voice. Then, Lord, help us to be obedient to give as You would have us give. Thank You, Lord.*

Amen.

Stand Up for Jesus

1. Stand up, stand up for Jesus! Ye sol - diers of the cross;
2. Stand up, stand up for Jesus! The trum - pet call o - bey;
3. Stand up, stand up for Jesus! Stand in His strength a - lone;
4. Stand up, stand up for Jesus! The strife will not be long;

Lift high His roy - al ban - ner, It must not suf - fer loss!
Forth to the might - y con - flict In this His glo - rious day;
The arm of flesh will fail you, Ye dare not trust your own;
This day the noise of bat - tle, The next the vic - tor's song;

From vic - t'ry un - to vic - t'ry His ar - my shall He lead,
Ye that are men now serve Him A - gainst un - num - bered foes;
Put on the gos - pel ar - mor, And watch - ing un - to prayer,
To Him that o - ver - com - eth A crown of life shall be;

Till ev - 'ry foe is van - quished, For Christ is Lord in - deed.
Let cour - age rise with dan - ger, And strength to strength op - pose.
Where du - ty calls, or dan - ger, Be nev - er want - ing there.
He with the King of Glo - ry Shall reign e - ter - nal - ly.

Stand Up for Jesus

LYRICS BY GEORGE DUFFIELD (1818–1888)
MUSIC BY GEORGE J. WEBB (1803–1887)

Stand therefore, having your loins girt about with truth, and having on the breastplate of righteousness; And your feet shod with the preparation of the gospel of peace; Above all, taking the shield of faith, wherewith ye shall be able to quench all the fiery darts of the wicked. And take the helmet of salvation, and the sword of the Spirit, which is the Word of God: Praying always with all prayer and supplication in the Spirit, and watching thereunto with all perseverance and supplication for all saints.
(Ephesians 6:14–18)

Episcopal minister Rev. Dudley Tyng was a dynamic young voice among the preachers participating in the Philadelphia revival of 1858. George Duffield, friend and admirer of Rev. Tyng, tells of "one of the most successful sermons of modern times" that Tyng delivered the Sunday before his death, at which, from an audience of five thousand, one thousand were saved.

Duffield tells of Tyng's untimely demise:

The following Wednesday, leaving his study for a moment, he went to the barn floor, where a mule was at work on a horse-power, shelling corn. Patting him on the neck, the sleeve of his silk study gown caught in the cogs of the wheel, and his arm was torn out by the roots! His death occurred in a few hours.[44]

Dudley tells us that Rev. Tyng's last words were, "'Tell them to stand up for Jesus.'... It was thought that these words had a peculiar significance in his mind; as if he had said, 'Stand up for Jesus in the person of the downtrodden slave.'"[45] These dying words inspired the composer of this hymn.

Prayer

Dear Jesus, let us in every situation know how to stand up for You. Teach us to hear the voice of the Holy Spirit in our hearts, that our actions might reflect Your character as we face every challenge of our lives. Thank You, Jesus.

Amen.

Standing on the Promises

1. Stand - ing on the prom - is - es of Christ my King, Thru e - ter - nal ag - es
2. Stand - ing on the prom - is - es that can - not fail, When the howl - ing storms of
3. Stand - ing on the prom - is - es of Christ the Lord, Bound to Him e - ter - nal -

let His prais - es ring; Glo - ry in the high - est, I will shout and sing,
doubt and fear as - sail, By the liv - ing word of God I shall pre - vail,
ly by love's strong cord, O - ver - com - ing dai - ly with the Spir - it's sword,

Chorus

Stand-ing on the prom-is-es of God. Stand - ing, stand - ing,
Stand-ing on the prom-is-es, stand-ing on the prom-is-es,

Stand - ing on the prom - is - es of God my Sav - ior; Stand - ing,
Stand - ing on the prom - is - es,

stand - ing, I'm stand - ing on the prom - is - es of God.
stand - ing on the prom - is - es,

Standing on the Promises

LYRICS AND MUSIC BY RUSSELL KELSO CARTER (1849–1928)

The grass withereth, the flower fadeth:
but the Word of our God shall stand for ever.
(Isaiah 40:8)

At the age of thirty, Russell Kelso Carter was faced with a health crisis without hope of a cure. He turned to God at that time, and this led to a life fully submitted to the service of the Lord. Here Carter describes what happened:

> Seven years ago he [Carter, speaking in the third person] was healed of a stubborn case of organic heart disease, after the best physicians and the most favorable climate and manner of life had alike signally failed to afford relief.... Jesus Christ has provided for believers the possibility of deliverance from the inward power of disease (as well as from sin).... Now we have seen that the promises of God most undeniably contain the assurance of physical health, on condition of obedience.... In [2 Corinthians 1:20], we read, *"For all the promises of God in Him are yea, and in Him Amen, unto the glory of God by us."*[46]

Sometimes a crisis of life-and-death proportions enters our lives, and we are tested in our faith. When "howling storms of doubt and fear assail," do we run to the Rock? Do we truly stand on God's promises and anchor ourselves on His holy Word? Russell Carter's health challenge was the turning point in life that brought him to a deeper level of faith through the storm. And God miraculously healed Carter and gave him forty-nine more years of vibrant good health!

"The Word of our God shall stand for ever" (Isaiah 40:8). The Word of God is the only place to stand that is unmovable, unshakable, solid, and eternal. "By the living Word of God I shall prevail."

Prayer

*Most excellent, glorious King of kings, thank You for an eternal place to stand where there is no sinking sand because we are **Standing on the Promises** of God.*

Amen.

Sweet By and By

1. There's a land that is fair - er than day, And by faith we can see
2. We shall sing on that beau - ti - ful shore The me - lo - di - ous songs
3. To our boun - ti - ful Fa - ther a - bove We will of - fer our trib-

it a - far; For the Fa - ther waits o - ver the way, To pre-
of the blest; And our spir - its shall sor - row no more— Not a
ute of praise For the glo - ri - ous gift of His love, And the

pare us a dwell - ing place there.
sigh for the bless - ings of rest.
bless - ings that hal - low our days.

Chorus

In the sweet by and
In the sweet

by, We shall meet on that beau - ti - ful shore; In the
by and by, by and by,

sweet by and by, We shall meet on that beau - ti - ful shore.
In the sweet by and by, by and by;

Sweet By and By

Lyrics by Sanford Fillmore Bennett (1836–1898)
Music by Joseph P. Webster (1819–1875)

Follow after charity, and desire spiritual gifts,
but rather that ye may prophesy.
(1 Corinthians 14:1)

Sanford Fillmore Bennett worked primarily in the medical field. He studied at Rush Medical College and ended up opening a drug store in Elkhorn, Wisconsin, which was also the home of composer Joseph P. Webster. Bennett describes writing **"Sweet By and By"** like this:

> Mr. Webster, like many musicians, was of an exceedingly nervous and sensitive nature, and subject to periods of depression, in which he looked upon the dark side of all things in life. I had learned his peculiarities so well that on meeting him I could tell at a glance if he was in one of his melancholy moods, and I found that I could rouse him from them by giving him a new song or hymn to work on. On such an occasion he came into my place of business, walked down to the stove, and turned his back to me without speaking. I was at my desk writing. Presently I said:
> "Webster, what is the matter now?"
> "It is no matter," he replied; "it will be all right by and by!"

"Like a flash of sunlight," the lyrics for **"Sweet By and By"** came to Bennett, and not more than thirty minutes later Webster had completed the music. With tears in his eyes, Webster proclaimed, "That hymn is immortal."[47]

Prayer

Dear Father, let us be spiritually aware when a friend has struggles, so that we may love our neighbor as ourselves. May we listen and hear as we seek answers through prayer, and then apply the gift of love to help them as we seek to follow Your Great Commandment, Lord. We respect You, Father, and we will not hold back in using our gifts from You to help others. Thank You, Lord.

Amen.

Sweet Hour of Prayer

1. Sweet hour of prayer! sweet hour of prayer, That calls me from a world of care,
2. Sweet hour of prayer! sweet hour of prayer, Thy wings shall my pe - ti - tion bear
3. Sweet hour of prayer! sweet hour of prayer, May I thy con - so - la - tion share

And bids me at my Fa - ther's throne Make all my wants and wish - es known;
To Him whose truth and faith - ful - ness En - gage the wait - ing soul to bless;
Till, from Mount Pis - gah's loft - y height, I view my home, and take my flight;

In sea - sons of dis - tress and grief, My soul has oft - en found re - lief,
And since He bids me seek His face, Be - lieve His word, and trust His grace,
This robe of flesh I'll drop, and rise To seize the ev - er - last - ing prize;

And oft es - caped the tempt-er's snare, By thy re - turn, sweet hour of prayer.
I'll cast on Him my ev - 'ry care, And wait for Thee, sweet hour of prayer.
And shout, while pass - ing thru the air, Fare - well, fare - well sweet hour of prayer.

Sweet Hour of Prayer

LYRICS BY WILLIAM W. WALFORD (1772–1850)
MUSIC BY WILLIAM B. BRADBURY (1816–1868)

But I say unto you, Love your enemies, bless them that curse you,
do good to them that hate you....
That ye may be the children of your Father which is in Heaven.
(Matthew 5:44–45)

R ev. Thomas Salmon tells the unusual story surrounding this hymn:

> I became acquainted with W. W. Walford, the blind preacher, a man
> of obscure birth and connections and no education, but of strong
> mind and most retentive memory. In the pulpit he never failed to
> select a lesson well adapted to his subject, giving chapter and verse
> with unerring precision...so as to have the reputation of "knowing
> the whole Bible by heart."
>
> On one occasion, paying him a visit, he repeated two or three
> pieces which he had composed, and having no friend at home to
> commit them to paper, he had laid them up in the storehouse with-
> in.... I rapidly copied the lines with my pencil, as he uttered them.[48]

Rev. Salmon asked the *New York Observer* to publish Walford's lines,
"if you should think them worthy of preservation." Indeed, they did,
and published them in 1845 alongside Salmon's story.

William B. Bradbury composed the music to Walford's lyrics.

We can all find relief in that special time we spend with the Lord, in
our "**Sweet Hour of Prayer**."

Prayer

*Thank You, Jesus, for teaching me by the Holy Spirit to look past the
flesh of a person and see into the heart, so that I will be able to see as
You do into their inner need. Then, Jesus, as I yield to You, may You
minister to their need through me.*

Amen.

Take the Name of Jesus with You

1. Take the name of Je - sus with you, Child of sor - row and of woe;
2. Take the name of Je - sus ev - er As a shield from ev - 'ry snare;
3. O the pre - cious name of Je - sus! How it thrills our souls with joy.

It will joy and com - fort give you, Take it then wher - e'er you go.
If temp - ta - tions 'round you gath - er, Breathe that ho - ly name in prayer.
When His lov - ing arms re - ceive us, And His songs our tongues em - ploy!

Chorus

Pre - cious name, O how sweet! Hope of earth and joy of heav'n;
Pre - cious name, O how sweet!

Pre - cious name, O how sweet! Hope of earth and joy of heav'n.
Pre - cious name, O how sweet, how sweet,

Take the Name of Jesus with You

LYRICS BY LYDIA BAXTER (1809–1874)
MUSIC BY WILLIAM HOWARD DOANE (1832–1915)

And when they saw Him, they worshipped Him: but some doubted.
And Jesus came and spake unto them, saying,
All power is given unto Me in heaven and in earth.
Go ye therefore, and teach all nations, baptizing them in the name
of the Father, and of the Son, and of the Holy Ghost.
(Matthew 28:17–19)

Through the years many trials have tested our faith. Right now you may feel dismayed, overwhelmed, desperate, vulnerable, without direction, and without protection.

Well, Christ Jesus is the answer. He has compassion for you and answers for your situation! Talk to Him, because, you see, there is nothing that you can't talk about with Him. Jesus sees your excitement, your tiredness, sadness, and happiness. So chatter away, because Jesus wants to share life with you. Otherwise, He wouldn't have died to save your life. Remember always, when you are tried and tested, Jesus is right there to get you through to victory!

Mrs. Lydia Baxter was bedridden for many years, but remained mentally active and even hosted meetings at her home. She loved studying the Bible and had a particular interest in the ancient Hebrew names and their meanings. When asked about how she maintained such a sunny attitude in the face of her physical obstacles, Lydia responded, "I have a very special armor. I have the name of Jesus. When the tempter tries to make me blue or despondent, I mention the name of Jesus, and he can't get through to me anymore. The name Jesus means 'Savior.'"[49] Lydia wrote **"Take the Name of Jesus with You"** only four years before she passed away.

Prayer

Sweet Jesus, Yours is the Name above every name, and there are times when I just don't know what else to pray, so I just speak Your Name. Thank You, Lord, that the Name of Jesus gives me power to overcome every situation.

Amen.

Tell Me the Story of Jesus

1. Tell me the story of Jesus, Write on my heart ev'ry word;
2. Fasting alone in the desert, Tell of the days that are past.
3. Tell of the cross where they nailed Him, Writhing in anguish and pain;

Fine

Tell me the story most precious, Sweetest that ever was heard;
How for our sins He was tempted, Yet was triumphant at last;
Tell of the grave where they laid Him, Tell how He liveth again.

D.S.— Tell me the story most precious, Sweetest that ever was heard.

Tell how the angels in chorus, Sang as they welcomed His birth;
Tell of the years of His labor, Tell of the sorrow He bore,
Love, in that story so tender, Clearer than ever I see;

"Glory to God in the highest! Peace and good tidings on earth."
He was despised and afflicted, Homeless, rejected and poor:
Stay, let me weep while you whisper, "Love paid the ransom for me."

Chorus

D.S. al Fine

Tell me the story of Jesus, Write on my heart ev'ry word:

Tell Me the Story of Jesus

Lyrics by Fanny J. Crosby (1820–1915)
Music by John R. Sweney (1837–1899)

For there is one God, and one mediator between God and men,
the man Christ Jesus; Who gave Himself a ransom for all,
to be testified in due time.
(1 Timothy 2:5–6)

When we look at all the belief systems in our world today, we can't help but notice that the Gospel of Jesus Christ is not high on the list of popular worldviews. Yet even as God's truth is denied in society, it still remains as the only remedy for the hopelessness of the human condition. We must tell the story of Jesus, otherwise the world may never learn that "Love paid the ransom for me." Are you willing to be that timid person who nevertheless speaks up in the midst of confusion and deception to proclaim the **Story of Jesus**?

God, who at sundry times and in divers manners spake in time past
unto the fathers by the prophets, hath in these last days spoken unto
us by His Son, whom He hath appointed heir of all things, by whom
also He made the worlds; Who being the brightness of His glory,
and the express image of His person, and upholding all things by the
word of His power, when He had by Himself purged our sins,
sat down on the right hand of the Majesty on high.
(Hebrews 1:1–3)

As is sometimes said, small steps each day can lead to huge changes! We must watch which way we go and whose steps we are following. Always check all words and actions by the Bible, the Word of God, before you follow.

Prayer

Lord Jesus, may we always follow after You. May we hear Your voice, the Holy Spirit within us, confirming that You are leading us. Another's voice we will not follow. Thank You, Lord.

Amen.

There Is a Balm in Gilead

There is a balm in Gil-e-ad to make the wound-ed whole;

There is a balm in Gil-e-ad to heal the sin-sick soul.

Fine

1. Some - times I feel dis-cour-aged, And think my work's in vain, But
2. If you can-not preach like Pe - ter, If you can-not pray like Paul, you can

D.C. al Fine

then the Ho - ly Spir - it Re - vives my soul a - gain.
tell the love of Je - sus, And say, "He died for all."

There Is a Balm in Gilead

LYRICS AND MUSIC FROM AN AFRICAN AMERICAN SPIRITUAL

Is there no balm in Gilead; is there no physician there?
Why then is not the health of the daughter of my people recovered?
(Jeremiah 8:22)

What is a balm? It is a soothing healing ointment. The spiritual "There Is a Balm in Gilead" speaks of the soothing healing power of God. It is based on Jeremiah 8:22, in which the weeping prophet asks the poignant question, *"Is there no balm in Gilead; is there no physician there?"* Jeremiah cries out to his nation Israel, *"In vain shalt thou use many medicines; for thou shalt not be cured. The nations have heard of thy shame, and thy cry hath filled the land: for the mighty man hath stumbled against the mighty, and they are fallen both together"* (Jeremiah 46:11–12).

But yet, though Jeremiah asks this question in despair that his people are so far from recognizing the Balm of Gilead that is the Lord, the composers of this spiritual turn Jeremiah's question into a bold statement of faith. Howard Thurman writes, "The slave caught the mood of this spiritual dilemma, and with it did an amazing thing. He straightened the question mark in Jeremiah's sentence into an exclamation point: 'There Is a Balm in Gilead!' Here is a note of creative triumph."[50]

We read further, "This revised Gospel coincided with [the African American slaves'] hopes for freedom, which were reinforced whenever they sang about their God who they believed would do for them what God had done for the Israelites."[51]

May the balm that is the shed blood of Jesus Christ be your healing balm, restoring both body and spirit.

Prayer

Dear Jesus, our supernatural Savior, we praise You for people who truly believe Your Word. You went to the depths of the earth to save us. You bore lashes on Your back and shed Your blood as a healing balm for us. We love You for exercising Your supernatural power.

Amen.

There Is a Fountain

1. There is a foun-tain filled with blood, Drawn from Im-man-uel's veins;
2. Dear dy-ing Lamb, Thy pre-cious blood Shall nev-er lose its pow'r,
3. E'er since, by faith, I saw the stream Thy flow-ing wounds sup - ply,

And sin-ners, plunged be-neath that flood, Lose all their guilt-y stains.
Till all the ran-somed church of God Be saved, to sin no more.
Re - deem-ing love has been my theme And shall be till I die.

Lose all their guilt-y stains, Lose all their guilt - y stains;
Be saved, to sin no more, Be saved, to sin no more;
And shall be till I die, And shall be till I die;

And sin-ners plunged be-neath that flood, Lose all their guilt-y stains.
Till all the ran-somed church of God Be saved, to sin no more.
Re - deem-ing love has been my theme, And shall be till I die.

There Is a Fountain

Lyrics by William Cowper (1731–1800)
Music: Traditional American Melody

*But now in Christ Jesus ye who sometimes were far off
are made nigh by the blood of Christ.*
(Ephesians 2:13)

*The law of the wise is a fountain of life,
to depart from the snares of death.*
(Proverbs 13:14)

Jesus was so brutally beaten and shed so much blood during His scourging that He became almost unrecognizable. His flesh was torn from His body. He was so weakened by loss of blood on the Via Dolorosa, on the way to Mount Golgotha, that He could no longer carry the cross.

"**There Is a Fountain** filled with blood, drawn from Immanuel's veins; And sinners plunged beneath that flood, lose all their guilty stains." The second stanza of this hymn speaks of Jesus' death. "Dear dying Lamb, Thy precious blood shall never lose its power, till all the ransomed church of God be saved, to sin no more."

Have you, a family member, or friend experienced emotional melancholy, mental depression, or spiritual doubt? There is an answer! All that Jesus suffered was for our healing! Does the description of the Passion of Jesus make you squeamish? Well, He suffered this painful and terrible death on the cross for you and for me. You know, Jesus had a choice, and He chose His love for you and me over His own comfort. He gave up His life to save ours. Now we may make our choice for obedience, with the hope of eternal life in everlasting peace, praise, health, joy, and beauty. Jesus is the Light, and where He is, there is no night. The lion will lie down by the lamb. *Praise the Lord Jesus—praise His Holy Name!*

Prayer

Most Holy Lord, we praise You for opening our eyes, so we may see how rich and matchless is Your precious blood. Forever, Lord, we will honor Your blood!

Amen.

There Is Power in the Blood

1. Would you be free from the bur - den of sin? There's pow'r in the blood,
2. Would you be free from your pas - sion and pride? There's pow'r in the blood,
3. Would you be whit - er, much whit - er than snow? There's pow'r in the blood,
4. Would you do ser - vice for Je - sus your King? There's pow'r in the blood,

pow'r in the blood; Would you o'er e - vil a vic - to - ry win? There's
pow'r in the blood; Come for a cleans - ing to Cal - va - ry's tide; There's
pow'r in the blood; Sin - stains are lost in its life - giv - ing flow; There's
pow'r in the blood; Would you live dai - ly His prais - es to sing? There's

Chorus

There is pow'r, pow'r, Won - der work - ing pow'r
won - der - ful pow'r in the blood.

there is pow'r,

In the blood of the Lamb; There is pow'r, pow'r,
In the blood of the Lamb; there is pow'r,

Won - der work - ing pow'r In the pre - cious blood of the Lamb.

There Is Power in the Blood

LYRICS AND MUSIC BY LEWIS E. JONES (1865–1936)

*For the life of the flesh is in the blood: and I have given it to you
upon the altar to make an atonement for your souls:
for it is the blood that maketh an atonement for the soul.*
(Leviticus 17:11)

Some people these days are seeking to eliminate the mention of the shed blood of Jesus Christ from our hymnals. This trend is inspired by the enemy of our souls. Do these people not know that such an accommodation of the flesh would take away our redemption? Jesus shed His royal blood at Calvary so that we may experience grace, be saved, and be redeemed from the curse of the law of sin and death. He died to give us life—not only this earthly life, which is just for a short time, but life throughout eternity in heaven, a place of joy unspeakable.

You know, without our blood flowing through our veins, we would be dead! Likewise, without the shed blood of our Savior, bringing salvation and redemption through Jesus Christ's death on the cross in our place, we would have to suffer and die for ourselves, bearing the unbearable burden of our own sins.

What a loving gift of life God gave us through Jesus, our Redeemer! He took our place, for **There Is Power in the Blood**! Yes, through His shed blood there is power.

I believe we should leave these hymns the way God's inspiration caused the lyricists to write them. These hymns bring the knowledge of victory in the blood of Jesus Christ, our Lord.

"Behold, I give unto you power to tread on serpents and scorpions, and over all the power of the enemy: and nothing shall by any means hurt you" (Luke 10:19). We have authority over the enemy, to use in the Name of Jesus and to the glory of God.

Prayer

*Dear God, I praise You that **There Is Power in the Blood** of the Lamb—power enough to bring the whole world to the saving knowledge of Jesus Christ. Please continue to empower us to speak to people about Your blood and to lead them to Christ's great gift of salvation through the shed blood of Jesus.*

Amen.

'Tis So Sweet to Trust in Jesus

1. 'Tis so sweet to trust in Je - sus, Just to take Him at His Word,
2. O how sweet to trust in Je - sus, Just to trust His cleans - ing blood,
3. Yes, 'tis sweet to trust in Je - sus, Just from sin and self to cease,
4. I'm so glad I learned to trust Thee, Pre-cious Je - sus, Sav - ior, Friend;

Just to rest up - on His prom - ise, Just to know, "Thus says the Lord."
Just in sim - ple faith to plunge me 'Neath the heal - ing, cleans-ing flood.
Just from Je - sus sim - ply tak - ing Life and rest, and joy and peace.
And I know that Thou art with me, Wilt be with me to the end.

Chorus

Je - sus, Je - sus, how I trust Him! How I've proved Him o'er and o'er!

Je - sus, Je - sus, pre - cious Je - sus! O for grace to trust Him more!

'Tis So Sweet to Trust in Jesus

LYRICS BY LOUISA M. R. STEAD (1850–1917)
MUSIC BY WILLIAM J. KIRKPATRICK (1838–1921)

Though He slay me, yet will I trust in Him.
(Job 13:15)

*Cause me to hear Thy lovingkindness in the morning; for in Thee
do I trust: cause me to know the way wherein I should walk;
for I lift up my soul unto Thee.*
(Psalm 143:8)

*L*ouisa received Jesus as her Savior at the age of nine. At the age of twenty-one Louisa felt the strong call of God on her life to become a missionary. In 1875 she married, and very soon was born a darling daughter named Lily.

We read the following tragic story about what befell the Stead family in *101 More Hymn Stories*:

> When the child was four years of age, the family decided one day to enjoy the sunny beach at Long Island Sound, New York. While eating their picnic lunch, they suddenly heard cries of help and spotted a drowning boy in the sea. Mr. Stead charged into the water. As often happens, however, the struggling boy pulled his rescuer under the water with him, and both drowned before the terrified eyes of wife and daughter.

> Such a wonderful day ended in such tragedy.

It is very fitting that a missionary would write this hymn about faith and trust in God. In spite of uncertainty and adversity, Louisa found "life and rest, and joy and peace." Soon after their loss, Louisa and Lily became missionaries to South Africa. Louisa met and eventually married Robert Wodehouse during her fifteen years there.

Louisa once wrote, "…one cannot, in the face of the peculiar difficulties, help say, 'Who is sufficient for these things?' But with simple confidence and trust we may and do say, 'Our sufficiency is of God.'"[52]

Prayer

Thank You, Lord, for purposeful callings, for each of Your children. May we be strong enough to consistently follow Your will, through all the days of our lives.

Amen.

To God Be the Glory

1. To God be the glo - ry, great things He hath done; So loved He the
2. O per - fect re - demp - tion, the pur - chase of blood; To ev - 'ry be-
3. Great things He hath taught us, great things He hath done, And great our re-

world that He gave us His Son, Who yield - ed His life an a-
liev - er the prom - ise of God; The vil - est of - fend - ers who
joic - ing thru Je - sus the Son; But pur - er, and high - er, and

tone - ment for sin, And o - pened the life - gate that all may go in.
tru - ly o - bey, That mo - ment from Je - sus a par - don re - ceives.
great - er will be Our won - der, our trans - port, when Je - sus we see.

Chorus

Praise the Lord, praise the Lord, Let the earth hear His voice! Praise the Lord,
praise the Lord,

Let the peo - ple re - joice! O come to the Fa - ther, thru

Je - sus the Son, And give Him the glo - ry, great things He hath done.

To God Be the Glory

Lyrics by Fanny J. Crosby (1820–1915)
Music by William Howard Doane (1832–1915)

The Lord hath done great things for us; whereof we are glad.
(Psalm 126:3)

Fanny was blind since she was an infant. Yet she composed over eight thousand hymns, becoming known as America's best writer of hymns. Fanny was born in New York, and at age fifteen she attended New York Institute for the Education of the Blind. Fanny became aware of her skill for writing lyric poetry, and her talent increased. Her accomplishment for writing secular songs became evident. She wrote "Rosalie, the Prairie Flower," which sold more than 125,000 copies.

In 1858 Fanny married Alexander van Alstyne, a musician who was also blind. Six years later they met William B. Bradbury, a famous composer, and at his request she wrote her first hymn. With that, Fanny felt that she had found her life's calling, saying, "I am the happiest creature in all the land." **To God Be the Glory!**

Fanny Crosby was ninety-five years of age when she passed away. Fanny took her gift and used it for God. Maybe we should all think on her attitude toward her circumstances: in spite of her blindness she had a wonderful attitude. Through knowing Christ, God's character developed in her, enabling her to overcome her condition. **To God Be the Glory** that we too can know God in this way! We too are capable of taking up the gifts we are given and blessing the kingdom of God with them.

You may be thinking, what is my gift? Love is the greatest gift, for it is—in whatever way you are talented—a gift we may share, as God did! "So loved He the world that He gave us His Son, Who yielded His life an atonement for sin, and opened the life-gate that all may go in."

Prayer

Thank You, Lord, that You gave Your life, and that if we ask, salvation is free to us. You took lashes from a whip on Your back so that we may be healed, then You gave us life eternal and a home in heaven with You forever. Thank You, Jesus.

Amen.

Trust and Obey

1. When we walk with the Lord In the light of His Word, What a glo - ry He
2. Not a shad - ow can rise, Not a cloud in the skies, But His smile quick - ly
3. Not a bur - den we bear, Not a sor - row we share, But our toil He doth
4. But we nev - er can prove The de - lights of His love Un - til all on the
5. Then in fel - low - ship sweet We will sit at His feet, Or we'll walk by His

sheds on our way! While we do His good will, He a - bides with us still,
drives it a - way; Not a doubt nor a fear, Not a sigh nor a tear,
rich - ly re - pay; Not a grief nor a loss, Not a frown nor a cross,
al - tar we lay; For the fa - vor He shows, And the joy He be - stows,
side in the way; What He says we will do, Where He sends we will go—

Chorus

And with all who will trust and o - bey.
Can a - bide while we trust and o - bey.
But is blest if we trust and o - bey. Trust and o - bey, for there's
Are for those who will trust and o - bey.
Nev - er fear, on - ly trust and o - bey.

no oth - er way To be hap - py in Je - sus, but to trust and o - bey.

Trust and Obey

LYRICS BY JOHN H. SAMMIS (1846–1919)
MUSIC BY DANIEL B. TOWNER (1850–1919)

*But He said, Yea rather, blessed are they
that hear the Word of God, and keep it.*
(Luke 11:28)

*For ye were sometimes darkness, but now are ye light in the Lord:
walk as children of light: (For the fruit of the Spirit
is in all goodness and righteousness and truth;)
Proving what is acceptable unto the Lord.*
(Ephesians 5:8–10)

*Y*ou know, in this modern life in the United States, we drive too fast and eat too much. We drink too many energy drinks, caffeinated sodas, and specialty coffees—wine, hard liquor, and so on—well, you get the idea. Many times we go from our job or a shopping trip to our vehicle, almost without thinking. We cross a parking lot or a street not really aware of what we are doing. Yes, when we are running on autopilot, we sometimes forget to obey the law. We move our vehicle without looking or cruise past a stop sign without stopping. We trust all will be well as long as no one sees us.

Even if no human saw us, we did not obey the law of the land. We knew what was right but deliberately did not obey. Well now, what about our spiritual obedience? Do we love ourselves more than God? The refrain of this song causes us to face ourselves about our obedience. "**Trust and Obey**, for there's no other way to be happy in Jesus, but to **Trust and Obey.**"

Let us stop and think about what we are doing and then purpose in our hearts and lives to obey the law and obey God. We are free to choose, but we are not free from the consequences of our choices. In Mark 12:17 it says, "*And Jesus answering said unto them, Render to Caesar the things that are Caesar's, and to God the things that are God's. And they marvelled at Him.*"

Prayer

Father, we ask You for forgiveness where we have failed to obey. We love You, Lord, and know that obeying will bring richness to our souls.

Amen.

The Unclouded Day

1. O they tell me of a home far be - yond the skies, O they
2. O they tell me of a home where the saints have gone, O they
3. O they tell me that He smiles on His chil - dren there, And His

tell me of a home far a - way; O they tell me of a home where no
tell me of that land far a - way, Where the tree of life in e -
smile drives their sor - rows all a - way; And they tell me that no tears ev - er

D.S.— O they tell me of a home where no

Fine

storm clouds rise, O they tell me of an un - cloud - ed day.
ter - nal bloom Sheds its fra - grance thru the un - cloud - ed day.
come a - gain, In that love - ly land of un - cloud - ed day.

storm clouds rise, O they tell me of an un - cloud - ed day.

Chorus

D.S. al Fine

O the land of cloud - less day, O the land of an un - cloud - ed sky;

190

The Unclouded Day

LYRICS AND MUSIC BY J. K. ALWOOD (1828–1909)

*And hath raised us up together, and made us sit together
in heavenly places in Christ Jesus.*
(Ephesians 2:6)

Josiah Kelly Alwood was a circuit-riding preacher who made regular rounds of the churches of rural Ohio on horseback. Heading homeward on one brilliant night ride after weeks away from his family, Alwood became inspired with the words of this hymn. As soon as he returned home, he woke up his wife and sang the new song for her.

We read, "Perhaps because of the song's direct, elemental, and rather straightforward style, few city churches latched onto it. Yet the fact that the song was unsophisticated and that it seemed meant to be sung in clear air while viewing nature's majesty probably kept it from being lost in the back of dusty hymnals."[53]

*Sing unto the LORD with thanksgiving; sing praise upon the harp
unto our God: who covereth the heaven with clouds, who prepareth
rain for the earth, who maketh grass to grow upon the mountains.*
(Psalm 147: 7–8)

*In Thy presence is fulness of joy;
at Thy right hand there are pleasures for evermore.*
(Psalm 16:11)

What are the clouds in your life today? Do sickness, sadness, sorrow, terror, or trouble interfere with your vision of heaven? You know all those adversities will be gone one day, and there will only be peace, joy, and love in our forever heavenly home.

Prayer

Father, when we envision heaven, we see You. Just knowing we will be with You for eternity brings unspeakable gladness. One day we will have all our questions answered. We praise Your miraculous Name! We have liberty to praise You timelessly, forever more.

Amen.

.

.

.

We Gather Together

1. We gather together to ask the Lord's blessing, He chastens and hastens His will to make known; The wicked oppressing now cease from distressing: Sing praises to His Name— He fails not His own!

2. Beside us to guide us, our God with us joining, Ordaining, maintaining His kingdom divine; So from the beginning the fight we were winning: Lord, Thine be all the glory— The vic'try is Thine!

3. We all do extol Thee, Thou King of the nation; And pray that Thou still our Defender wilt be; May Thy congregation escape tribulation: Be Thou for ever praised, Thou God of the free!

"We Gather Together" Family Worship, Jean-Baptiste Greuze (1725–1805)

We Gather Together

ANONYMOUS DUTCH HYMN
TRANSLATED BY THEODORE BAKER (1851–1934)

And be not drunk with wine, wherein is excess; but be filled with the Spirit; speaking to yourselves in psalms and hymns and spiritual songs, singing and making melody in your heart to the Lord.
(Ephesians 5:18–19)

At Thanksgiving, family members and friends gather together for a delicious traditional meal of turkey with all the trimmings from special family recipes. Nourishing and fragrant dishes are passed around the table, while prayers of thanksgiving are lifted to God. This year, go around the table and ask each person to share about what they are thankful for.

While I was in my formative years, my pastor was my own father, Rev. S. Boyd McSpadden, a minister of the Gospel. He loved to quote Ephesians 5:20: *"Giving thanks always for all things unto God and the Father in the name of our Lord Jesus Christ."*

This song dates back to the struggle of the Dutch Protestants of the late 1500s against the persecution brought upon them by the Spanish king Phillip II. The Dutch sought to preserve their form of Christian worship in the face of Spanish prohibition and were victorious, by God's grace. The melody was taken from a traditional folk song, while the words speak of how God brought them through to freedom: "He chastens and hastens His will to make known; The wicked oppressing now cease from distressing."

"**We Gather Together**" journeyed with the Dutch settlers to the American continent in the 1620s, and American music scholar Theodore Baker translated it into English in 1894.

Prayer

*Jesus, we come with praise and thanksgiving for this nation made up of all the peoples of the world, and we pray that America will again gather together to give thanks. For we know You have provided blessings each day for us, for America, our President, and all who help to govern. Lord, let peace reign on earth as **We Gather Together** as one.*

Amen.

We're Marching to Zion

We're Marching to Zion

Lyrics by Isaac Watts (1674–1748)
Music by Robert Lowry (1826–1899)

*For there shall be a day, that the watchmen upon
the mount Ephraim shall cry, Arise ye,
and let us go up to Zion unto the Lord our God.*
(Jeremiah 31:6)

Isaac Watts wrote this song about coming together as the body of Christ, joining together "in a song with sweet accord" and marching toward our goal, which is heaven—our eternal home!

We are soldiers in the army of the Lord. We are training to be fit and able to take our orders and follow through. "*He that overcometh shall inherit all things; and I will be his God, and he shall be My son*" (Revelation 21:7). I really cling to this chapter, for it says, "*And God shall wipe away all tears from their eyes; and there shall be no more death, neither sorrow, nor crying, neither shall there be any more pain: for the former things are passed away*" (Revelation 21:4).

When my daughter Cherie was born, it was the most joyous day. She was small and thin because she was born five weeks early. When the doctor came in, he said, "You have a beautiful baby girl." However, he didn't stop there. "We have an issue, so for the next few hours ask your father, the Reverend Boyd McSpadden, to help you pray, because I know your family believes in miracles." Then the doctor continued, "The baby has hyaline membrane disease. Her lungs are not completely developed. We have placed her in a machine that recreates, as closely as possible, the conditions in the birth sack. If she responds well it should only be a week or so, and with God's miracle, she will be able to go home."

With much prayer from all the people we knew that had faith in God our Father, she was healed, home, and healthy within ten days. *Praise God from whom all blessing flow!*

Prayer

Lord, thank You for giving us hope in this life, that heaven, the city of God, is prepared for us. We give You thanks that You never leave us, but go with us through every challenge of life.

Amen.

Were You There

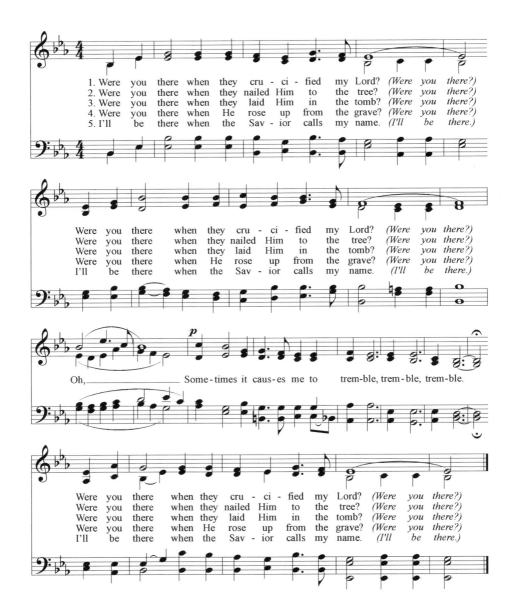

1. Were you there when they cru - ci - fied my Lord? *(Were you there?)*
2. Were you there when they nailed Him to the tree? *(Were you there?)*
3. Were you there when they laid Him in the tomb? *(Were you there?)*
4. Were you there when He rose up from the grave? *(Were you there?)*
5. I'll be there when the Sav - ior calls my name. *(I'll be there.)*

Were you there when they cru - ci - fied my Lord? *(Were you there?)*
Were you there when they nailed Him to the tree? *(Were you there?)*
Were you there when they laid Him in the tomb? *(Were you there?)*
Were you there when He rose up from the grave? *(Were you there?)*
I'll be there when the Sav - ior calls my name. *(I'll be there.)*

Oh, Some - times it caus - es me to trem - ble, trem - ble, trem - ble.

Were you there when they cru - ci - fied my Lord? *(Were you there?)*
Were you there when they nailed Him to the tree? *(Were you there?)*
Were you there when they laid Him in the tomb? *(Were you there?)*
Were you there when He rose up from the grave? *(Were you there?)*
I'll be there when the Sav - ior calls my name. *(I'll be there.)*

Were You There

LYRICS AND MUSIC FROM AFRICAN AMERICAN SPIRITUAL

Knowing this, that our old man is crucified with Him, that the body of sin might be destroyed, that henceforth we should not serve sin.
(Romans 6:6)

Imagine being in Jerusalem during the time of Jesus' crucifixion, burial, and resurrection. The very thought of a sinless, loving Jesus going to the cross with mocking and ridicule hurts me to the core. Imagine the contemptuous, dismissive behavior of the soldiers, as they spit at Jesus, slapped Him, and yelled, "King of the Jews!" Can you hear the rousing laughter, disdain, and anger? And for what reason? They took Jesus to the cross to hang there in disgrace, even though He was not guilty. They gave the notorious thief Barabbas freedom instead of our Lord Jesus. "Sometimes it causes me to tremble, tremble, tremble."

The devil thought he had his way at that time, but he didn't count on Jesus rising on the third day in victory! Jesus came out of the tomb, conquering death, hell, and the grave, as our soon-returning King.

In this African American spiritual we can see how Christian slaves in early America balanced suffering and hope. Arthur Jones writes, "The symbolism of the Jesus story and its message of better times ahead were explored most fully in songs about Jesus' death, and the opportunity provided to singers to identify with a life in which suffering offered the promise of redemption and salvation."[54]

Were You There? I was not there then, but I am eager to be there at His second coming, aren't you? *Hallelujah! Praise the Lamb! We thank You, Jesus, that You are the victor. You gave us victory as well when You rose up from the dead. You will take us with You, our King, to eternal peace, love, and joy in heaven.*

Prayer

Let's pray this together: Lord Jesus, I am a sinner. I want You to come into my life and my heart. Cleanse me from all sin and unrighteousness, and make me Your child. Teach me Your ways. I believe You. In the Name of Jesus I pray this.

Amen.

What a Friend We Have in Jesus

1. What a Friend we have in Je - sus, All our sins and griefs to bear;
2. Have we tri - als and temp - ta - tions? Is there trou-ble an - y - where?
3. Are we weak and heav - y lad - en, Cum-bered with a load of care?

What a priv - i - lege to car - ry Ev - 'ry-thing to God in prayer.
We should nev - er be dis - cour - aged, Take it to the Lord in prayer.
Pre - cious Sav - ior, still our ref - uge,— Take it to the Lord in prayer.

O what peace we of - ten for - feit, O what need - less pain we bear,
Can we find a Friend so faith - ful, Who will all our sor - rows share?
Do thy friends de - spise, for - sake thee? Take it to the Lord in prayer;

All be - cause we do not car - ry Ev - 'ry-thing to God in prayer.
Je - sus knows our ev - 'ry weak - ness: Take it to the Lord in prayer.
In His arms He'll take and shield thee; Thou wilt find a sol - ace there.

What a Friend We Have in Jesus

LYRICS BY JOSEPH MEDLICOTT SCRIVEN (1819–1886)
MUSIC BY CHARLES C. CONVERSE (1832–1918)

Henceforth I call you not servants; for the servant knoweth not what his lord doeth: but I have called you friends; for all things that I have heard of My Father I have made known unto you.
(John 15:15)

As I write this, a good friend from our church has been attacked by the enemy of our body with cancer. Cancer can be just a word that brings fear and doubt. But we have faith, and we have power in Jesus' Name to cast it out. The Bible says that according to our faith we will be made whole. The Bible also says that by Jesus' stripes we are healed. Now, those are two very faith-filled promises. Jesus took the thrashing and pain of a whip known as a *flagrum* on His back, for our healing.

But how do we have the faith of Jesus? As the song says, "Take it to the Lord in prayer." Some years ago, my sister-in-law Carol McSpadden was told she had cancer. Well, if you knew my sister-in-law you would know she would not just sit down and take the devil's dealings! She was bold in her faith and the promise of healing the Lord has given. When she returned home she closed the door and slammed her clenched fist on the table, proclaiming forcefully to satan, "You will not take my life, in the Name of Jesus! I am healed!" I believe she never looked back; she only moved forward toward her healing. Carol and my brother, Pastor Gary, placed Scriptures in front of her eyes and mind so she could continually speak them out loud and keep them foremost in her thoughts.

We all prayed and believed what God said: that she was already healed and what we had to do was *"to stand"* (Ephesians 6:13). *"Wherefore take unto you the whole armor of God, that ye may be able to withstand in the evil day, and having done all, to stand."*

Carol has been cancer free for more than five years and praises the Lord for her healing, giving her testimony of God's love and the healing power of standing in the faith of Jesus.

Prayer

You are our miracle-working Lord. We truly want to thank You for showing us how to fight the enemy by praying, believing, and standing in the powerful Name of Jesus—our Healer—by faith. Amen.

When I Survey the Wondrous Cross

1. When I sur - vey the won - drous cross On which the
2. For - bid it, Lord, that I should boast, Save in the
3. See, from His head, His hands, His feet, Sor - row and
4. Were the whole realm of na - ture mine, That were a

Prince of glo - ry died, My rich - est gain I
death of Christ, my Lord; All the vain things that
love flow min - gled down; Did e'er such love and
pre - sent far too small; Love so a - maz - ing,

count but loss, And pour con - tempt on all my pride.
charm me most, I sac - ri - fice them to His blood.
sor - row meet, Or thorns com - pose so rich a crown?
so di - vine, De - mands my soul, my life, my all.

When I Survey the Wondrous Cross

Lyrics by Isaac Watts (1674–1748)
Music by Lowell Mason (1792–1872)

I am crucified with Christ: nevertheless I live; yet not I, but Christ liveth in me: and the life which I now live in the flesh I live by the faith of the Son of God, who loved me, and gave Himself for me.
(Galatians 2:20)

Without the cross of Jesus we would have no forgiveness of sins, and we would not know the riches of His grace. But the "Prince of glory" died for us, to remove pride, prejudice, confusion, division, hatred, rebellion, lust, murder, and any other wrong that our flesh under satanic rule or persuasion can produce. Jesus came to give life and that more abundantly, so we can live in love, peace, joy, and happiness together with others.

When we accept Jesus as our Savior, we may live in expectation of the goodness of the miracle plan God has for our lives. **When I Survey the Wondrous Cross,** I praise God, from whom all blessings flow. We have hope for new days, vision for God's plan, and pleasure in obedience and righteousness. We bear fruit for the kingdom of heaven.

Lord, You are our life and our daily cause for celebration, because we know that You make all things new. Every morning when I arise to a sunny day or new-mown hay, the sweet smell of rain or life's new challenge, I know You are the answer to any question I may have.

When I call on the Lord in the light of His love, He tenderly speaks to my heart in that still, small voice of love. I am so grateful He is there!

Prayer

I thank You, dear Lord God, for Your sweet whisper of hope when I am sad from loss. Your peace covers the turmoil that sometimes surrounds us, Your power overcomes what we face at times. Your gentle ways dry all our tears. Forgive us when we fail to call on You when we need Your support and answers. We love You, for You care for us, You are our Holy Father, and we are loved by You! Thank You, dear Lord.

Amen.

When the Roll Is Called Up Yonder

1. When the trum-pet of the Lord shall sound and time shall be no more,
2. On that bright and cloud-less morn-ing when the dead in Christ shall rise,
3. Let us la-bor for the Mas-ter from the dawn till set-ting sun,

And the morn-ing breaks e-ter-nal, bright and fair; When the saved of earth shall gath-er
And the glo-ry of His res-ur-rec-tion share; When His cho-sen ones shall gath-er
Let us talk of all His won-drous love and care; Then when all of life is o-ver

o-ver on the oth-er shore, And the
to their home be-yond the skies, And the roll is called up yon-der, I'll be there.
and our work on earth is done, And the

Fine

Chorus

When the roll is called up yon - der, When the roll is
When the roll is called up yon-der I'll be there, When the roll is

called up yon - - der, When the roll is called up yon-der, When the
called up yon-der I'll be there, When the roll is called up yon-der,

D.S. al Fine

When the Roll Is Called Up Yonder

LYRICS AND MUSIC BY JAMES M. BLACK (1856–1938)

*And I saw the dead, small and great, stand before God;
and the books were opened: and another book was opened,
which is the book of life: and the dead were judged out of those
things which were written in the books, according to their works.*
(Revelation 20:12)

*For the Lord Himself shall descend from heaven with a shout,
with the voice of the archangel, and with the trump of God:
and the dead in Christ shall rise first.*
(1 Thessalonians 4:16–17)

The composer of this hymn, James M. Black, tells us in his own words how this hymn came about:

While a teacher in a Sunday-school and president of a young people's society,…I one day met a girl, fourteen years old, poorly clad and the child of a drunkard. She accepted my invitation to attend the Sunday-school, and joined the young people's society. One evening at a consecration-meeting, when members answered the roll-call by repeating Scripture texts, she failed to respond. I spoke of what a sad thing it would be, when our names are called from the Lamb's Book of Life, if one of us should be absent; and I said, "O God, when my own name is called up yonder, may I be there to respond!" I longed for something suitable to sing just then, but I could find nothing in the books.… The thought came to me, "Why don't you make it?" I dismissed the idea, thinking that I could never write such a hymn. When I reached my house my wife saw that I was deeply troubled, and questioned me, but I made no reply. Then the words of the first stanza came to me in full. In fifteen minutes more I had composed the other two verses. Going to the piano, I played the music just as it is found to-day in the hymn-books.[55]

Prayer

Lord Jesus, please forgive me of the sins in my life, and make me clean by Your shed blood, so that when God's roll is called up yonder, I'll be there. Thank You, Jesus, for Your forgiveness and my redemption and salvation.

Amen.

When We All Get to Heaven

1. Sing the won-drous love of Je - sus, Sing His mer - cy and His grace:
2. While we walk the pil - grim path-way, Clouds will o - ver-spread the sky;
3. Let us then be true and faith - ful, Trust - ing, serv - ing ev - 'ry day;

In the man - sions bright and bless - ed, He'll pre - pare for us a place.
But when trav - 'ling days are o - ver, Not a shad-ow, not a sigh.
Just one glimpse of Him in glo - ry Will the toils of life re - pay.

Chorus

When we all get to heav - en, What a day of re - joic - ing
When we all What a day

that will be! When we all see Je - sus,
of re - joic - ing that will be! When we all

We'll sing and shout the vic - to - ry.
and shout the vic - to - ry.

When We All Get to Heaven

LYRICS BY ELIZA E. HEWITT (1851–1920)
MUSIC BY EMILY D. WILSON (1865–1942)

*That whosoever believeth in Him
should not perish, but have eternal life.*
(John 3:15)

School teacher Eliza Edmunds Hewitt, born June 28, 1851, collaborated with Emily Wilson, the wife of the Philadelphia Methodist District Superintendent, in the writing of this hymn. These two women wanted to share the Gospel with children, so that is where they sowed their best seed. Sow your good seed into the Kingdom of God.

What am I sowing? I must sow what I want to grow!

• Don't sow bad seed, such as judgment. Judge not that you be not judged; similarly, sow good seed bountifully.

• Reading God's holy Word will produce in you real and righteous fruit.

• If you sow honor to God, He will honor you. How? God shows you honor with His presence, daily leading you.

• When you speak the name of God or Jesus to others, listen for the Lord God in your heart, for He may speak to you with an answer and direction for them.

• "*Give, and it shall be given unto you*" (Luke 6:38). The tithe is God's ten percent of your earnings, and anything further given is an offering to God. We give, not out of duty, but because we love Him.

• Honor your family—your mother and father—doing what you can to protect and help them financially. This includes natural as well as spiritual parents!

In John 12 we read that Judas Iscariot tried to shame Mary for giving expensive perfume to the Lord. He did not value giving to the Lord Jesus, but was upset at what he saw as the waste of the ointment poured on Jesus' feet. Give God your best, as He has given His best to us.

Prayer

Lord, thank You for teaching us that we must do what You have designed us to do for success. I know that "I must sow what I want to grow." Thank You, Lord Jesus.

Amen.

Where He Leads I'll Follow

1. Sweet are the prom - is - es, Kind is the word; Dear - er far than
2. Sweet is the ten - der love Je - sus hath shown, Sweet - er far than
3. List to His lov - ing words, "Come un - to Me!" Wea - ry, heav - y -

an - y mes - sage man ev - er heard; Pure was the mind of Christ,
an - y love that mor - tals have known; Kind to the err - ing one,
lad - en, there is sweet rest for thee; Trust in His prom - is - es,

Sin - less, I see; He the great ex - am - ple is, and pat - tern for me.
Faith - ful is He; He the great ex - am - ple is, and pat - tern for me.
Faith - ful and sure; Lean up - on the Sav - ior and thy soul is se - cure.

Chorus

Where He leads I'll fol - low,
Where He leads I'll fol - low, Where He leads I'll fol - low,

1. Fol - low all the way;
Fol - low all the way, yes, fol - low all the way;
2. Fol - low Je - sus ev - 'ry day.

Where He Leads I'll Follow

LYRICS AND MUSIC BY WILLIAM A. OGDEN (1841–1897)

*The LORD is my shepherd; I shall not want. He maketh me to lie
down in green pastures: He leadeth me beside the still waters.
He restoreth my soul: He leadeth me in the paths of righteousness for
His name's sake. Yea, though I walk through the valley of the
shadow of death, I will fear no evil: for Thou art with me;
Thy rod and Thy staff they comfort me.*
(Psalm 23:1–4)

In years gone by, people farmed their land themselves. They would put a collar around the neck of the horse or whatever animal they used and then hold the two long handles which lead down to the plow blade and the animals' reigns. The blade of the plow would break up the ground, making a row. But if the animal started to turn to the left or to the right, it would pull the blade, and the row would not be straight. This would waste ground and time.

How many times has the Holy Spirit shown you the way you should go, but you were not paying enough attention, and you veered off the straight path that led to your goal? It is not always so easy to get back on track. There are things that can easily become habits that, without God's help, you cannot break! If you begin to take drugs or drink socially—and before you know it you are drinking too much—or if you are overtaken by the habit of gambling, you can lose your focus on the Lord's plan, missing the straight and narrow mark. It says in Philippians 3:14, "*I press toward the mark for the prize of the high calling of God in Christ Jesus.*"

If you keep your ears and eyes open, reading the Bible and hearing God's voice, you will not miss your calling, "*the eyes of your understanding being enlightened; that ye may know what is the hope of His calling*" (Ephesians 1:18a).

Prayer

Lord Jesus, we want to follow You where You lead us and to hear Your high calling as we press toward the mark for the prize, which is heaven—our goal. We love You and desire to do what You ask of us, in Jesus' Name.

Amen.

William Miller, 1872

Wonderful Grace of Jesus

LYRICS AND MUSIC BY HALDOR LILLENAS (1885–1959)

*And the grace of our Lord was exceeding abundant
with faith and love which is in Christ Jesus.*
(1 Timothy 1:14)

Jesus is our life giver; He is unrivaled, unequaled, incomparable, matchless, richly filling, overflowing with life to the ultimate maximum, and the same yesterday, today, and forever. Jesus is full of grace and truth!

*For he that soweth to his flesh shall of the flesh reap corruption; but
he that soweth to the Spirit shall of the Spirit reap life everlasting.*
(Galatians 6:8)

Haldor began learning how to sow good seed at an early age. He emigrated as a child from Norway. His family moved and finally settled in Oregon in 1889. He attended Bible college as well as music school, and earned an honorary Doctor of Music degree. Eventually, he became a pastor and was considered one of the major hymn writers of the last century, authoring approximately four thousand hymns. He was also a major publisher, with Lillenas Publishing Company.

Haldor married another songwriter named Bertha Mae Wilson and together they served in the Church of the Nazarene.

Haldor Lillenas sowed good seed all his life. His song "**Wonderful Grace of Jesus**" expresses how God loves and completely forgives because of His wonderful grace.

Prayer

God of grace, I thank You that Your grace is sufficient for all who repent and obey. Lord, You give us grace though we certainly don't deserve it. Thank You, gracious Father.

Amen.

Wonderful Grace of Jesus

1. Won-der-ful grace of Je-sus, Great-er than all my sin;
2. Won-der-ful grace of Je-sus, Reach-ing to all the lost,
3. Won-der-ful grace of Je-sus, Reach-ing the most de-filed,

How shall my tongue de-scribe it? Where shall its praise be-gin?
By it I have been par-doned, Saved to the ut-ter-most.
By its trans-form-ing pow-er Mak-ing him God's dear child,

Tak-ing a-way my bur-den, Set-ting my spir-it free;
Chains have been torn a-sun-der, Giv-ing me lib-er-ty;
Pur-chas-ing peace and heav-en, For all e-ter-ni-ty;

For the won-der-ful grace of Je-sus reach-es me.
For the won-der-ful grace of Je-sus reach-es me.
And the won-der-ful grace of Je-sus reach-es me.

Chorus

Won-der-ful the match-less grace, the match-less grace of Je-sus, Deep-er than the
Won-der-ful the match-less grace of Je-sus, Deep-er than the

Wonderful Grace of Jesus, *continued*

might - y roll - ing sea, the roll - ing sea; Won - - - der - ful
might - y roll - ing sea; High - er than the moun - tain,

grace all suf - fi - cient for
spark - ling like a foun - tain, All suf - fi - cient grace for e - ven

me, for e - ven me, Broad - er than the scope of my trans -
me, Broad - er than the scope of my trans -

gres - sions, Great - er far than all my sin and shame,
gres - sions, sing it! Great - er far than all my sin and shame, my sin and shame,

O mag - ni - fy the pre - cious name of Je - sus, Praise His name!

Wonderful Words of Life

1. Sing them o-ver a-gain to me, Won-der-ful words of Life;
2. Christ, the bless-ed One, gives to all, Won-der-ful words of Life;
3. Sweet-ly ech-o the gos-pel call, Won-der-ful words of Life;

Let me more of their beau-ty see, Won-der-ful words of Life.
Sin-ner, list to the lov-ing call, Won-der-ful words of Life.
Of-fer par-don and peace to all, Won-der-ful words of Life.

Words of life and beau-ty, Teach me faith and du-ty;
All so free-ly giv-en, Woo-ing us to heav-en;
Je-sus, on-ly Sav-ior, Sanc-ti-fy for-ev-er;

Chorus

Beau-ti-ful words, won-der-ful words, Won-der-ful words of Life;

Beau-ti-ful words, won-der-ful words, Won-der-ful words of Life.

Wonderful Words of Life

Lyrics and music by Philip P. Bliss (1838–1876)

*Jesus saith unto him, I am the way, the truth, and the life:
no man cometh unto the Father, but by Me.*
(John 14:6)

*It is the spirit that quickeneth; the flesh profiteth nothing:
the words that I speak unto you, they are spirit, and they are life.*
(John 6:63)

Your victory testimony is a continuous rebuke to the enemy and a constant reminder to him of his limited ability, and the awesome victory that Jesus won over him at Calvary! God's words are words of life to all who hear them. Choose life!

Reading the Bible, 1848
(Library of Congress, PD)

Prayer

Father, thank You for the glorious victory in Jesus won for us at Calvary. Now we have experienced victory and deliverance in our lives. Help us to continue to herald Christ's glorious ability to set all of us free!

Amen.

NOTES

1. G. K. Chesterton and Wyatt North, *Saint Francis of Assisi* (New York: G. H. Doran, 1924).

2. Rev. Duncan Morrison, *The Great Hymns of the Church* (Toronto: Hart & Co., 1890), 157–58.

3. John Julian, *A Dictionary of Hymnology* (New York: Charles Scribner's Sons, 1892), 238.

4. Fanny J. Crosby, *Fanny J. Crosby: An Autogiography* (Peabody, MA: Hendrickson Publishers, 2008), 176–77.

5. Robert Morgan, *Then Sings My Soul* (Nashville: Thomas Nelson, Inc., 2003), 183.

6. Julian, *A Dictionary of Hymnology*, 969–70.

7. Ernest Edwin Ryden, *The Story of Our Hymns* (Rock Island, IL: Augustana Book Concern, 1930), 178-79.

8. Charles Sumner Nutter and Wilbur Fisk Tillett, *The Hymns and Hymn Writers of the Church* (New York: Eaton & Mains, 1911), 437.

9. George MacDonald, *Cheerful Words* (Boston: D. Lothrop & Company, 1880), 15.

10. Emily Ruth Brink and Bertus Frederick Polman, *Psalter Hymnal Handbook* (Grand Rapids, MI: CRC Publications, 1998), 616.

11. Vincent D. Homan, *A Foot in Two Worlds: A Pastor's Journey from Grief to Hope* (Bloomington, IN: WestBow Press, 2013), 112.

12. Holmes and Co., *The Bengal Obituary* (London and Calcutta: W. Thacker & Co., 1851), p. 12.

13. Amos Russel Wells, *A Treasure of Hymns: Brief Biographies of One Hundred and Twenty Leading Hymn-Writers and Their Best Hymns* (Boston and Chicago: United Society of Christian Endeavor, 1914), 41.

14. Edith L. Blumhofer, *Her Heart Can See: The Life and Hymns of Fanny J. Crosby* (Grand Rapids: Eerdmans, 2005), 221–23.

15. Fanny Crosby, *Fanny Crosby's Life-story* (New York: Every Where Publishing Company, 1903), 14.

16. Ira David Sankey, *My Life and the Story of the Gospel Hymns* (Philadelphia: The Sunday School Times Company, 1906), 184–87.

17. Kenneth W. Osbeck, *101 More Hymn Stories* (Grand Rapids, MI: Kregel Publications, 1985), 133–34.

18. Wells, *A Treasure of Hymns*, 82–84.

19. Osbeck, *101 More Hymn Stories*, 136.

20. "C. Austin Miles," *Hymnary*, hymnary.org.

21. Shown on this page is the telegram from Anna Spafford to Horatio Gates Spafford re being "Saved alone" among her traveling party in the shipwreck of the Ville du Havre (American Colony in Jerusalem Papers, Manuscript Division, Library of Congress, Washington, D.C.).

22. Cliff Barrows and Donald Hustad, *Crusader Hymns and Hymn Stories*, Special Crusade Edition (Minneapolis: The Billy Graham Evangelistic Association, 1967), 25.

23. Ian Bradley, Daily Telegraph Book of Hymns (London: Continuum, 2005), 204.

24. Wells, *A Treasure of Hymns*, 49.

25. Ryden, *The Story of Our Hymns*.

26. Osbeck, *101 Hymn Stories* (Grand Rapids, MI: Kregel Publications, 1982), 144.

27. Warren W. Wiersbe, *Be Obedient: Learning the Secret of Living by Faith* (Colorado Springs: David C. Cook, 1991), 20.

28. Ira David Sankey, *My Life and Sacred Songs* (London: Hodder and Stoughton, 1906), 151.

29. Jacob Henry Hall, *Biography of Gospel Song and Hymn Writers* (Grand Rapids, MI: Fleming H. Revell, Co., 1914).

30. Morgan, *Then Sings My Soul*, 219.

31. Dwight L. Moody, "Let the Lower Lights Be Burning," sermoncentral.com.

32. Julian, *A Dictionary of Hymnology*, 698.

33. Kenneth W. Osbeck, *Amazing Grace: 366 Inspiring Hymn Stories for Daily Devotions* (Grand Rapids, MI: Kregel Publications, 2002), 46.

34. Morgan, *Then Sings My Soul*, 15.

35. Wells, *A Treasure of Hymns*, 72–75.

36. Julian, *A Dictionary of Hymnology*, 771.

37. Wells, *A Treasure of Hymns*, 55.

38. Julian, *A Dictionary of Hymnology*, 699.

39. Ryden, *The Story of Our Hymns*.

40. Dr. Stephen Flick, "George Bennard and The Old Rugged Cross," Christian Heritage Fellowship, christianheritagefellowship.com.

41. Osbeck, *101 Hymn Stories*, 255.

42. E. M. Long, *Illustrated History of Hymns and Their Authors* (Philadelphia: Joseph F. Jaggers, 1876), 64.

43. Kenneth W. Osbeck, *25 Most Treasured Gospel Hymn Stories* (Grand Rapids, MI: Kregel Publications, 1985), 57–58.

44. Samuel Willoughby Duffield (son of composer George Duffield), *English Hymns: Their Authors and History* (New York, London: Funk & Wagnalls, 1886), 494.

45. Julian, *A Dictionary of Hymnology*, 315.

46. Russell Kelso Carter, "Divine Healing, or 'Faith Cure,'" *The Century Illustrated Monthly Magazine*, vol. 33, November 1886 to April 1887, 777-780.

47. Sankey, *My Life and the Story of the Gospel Hymns*, 285–286.

48. *New York Observer*, September 13, 1845.

49. Osbeck, *101 More Hymn Stories*, 265.

50. Howard Thurman, *Deep River and The Negro Spiritual Speaks of Life and Death* (Richmond, IN: Friends United, 1975), 56.

51. Peter J. Paris, ed. with Julius Crump, *African American Theological Ethics* (Louisville, KY: Westminster John Knox Press, 2015), 295.

52. Osbeck, *101 More Hymn Stories*, 288.

53. Ace Collins, *Turn Your Radio On* (Grand Rapids: Zondervan, 1999).

54. Arthur Jones, *Wade in the Water: The Wisdom of the Spirituals* (Boulder, CO: Leave A Little Room, 2005), 31.

55. Sankey, *My Life and the Story of the Gospel Hymns*, 340–41.

New from Nordskog Publishing, Inc.

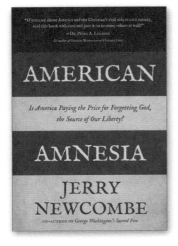
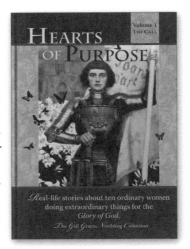

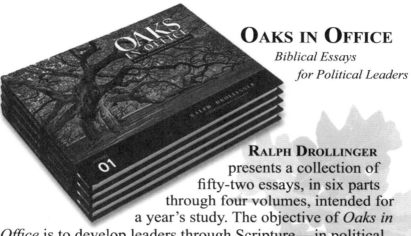
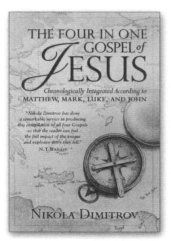